BRIDGE ANALYSIS

By BORIS SCHAPIRO

Introduction by
TERENCE REESE

STERLING PUBLISHING CO., INC. NEW YORK

Contents

© Boris Schapiro 1976
Published by Sterling Publishing Co., Inc.
419 Park Avenue South, New York, N.Y. 10016
Manufactured in the United States of America
Library of Congress Catalog Card No.: 76–1167
Sterling ISBN 0-8069-4928-7 Trade
4929-5 Library

Introduction

Short and to the point; that is Boris's style, well reflected in this book.

Wisely, I dare say, he sticks to bridge. While there is plenty of humour, it arises naturally from the hands he describes.

As everyone has a story about him, some readers may have expected more in the way of personal anecdotes. Here is one from the 1964 Olympiad in New York.

We were playing before a big gallery against a pair who frequently asked the meaning of our bids, however ordinary. At one point we were progressing towards a slam, answering questions on the way. Eventually Boris made a grand slam try of Six Diamonds, and after replying to the inevitable 'What do you understand by that?' I bid Seven No Trumps. Boris said quickly: 'That's a sign-off.'

It is not unknown for people to write introductions to books they have not read or even seen. To avert that charge, I venture to add a gloss to the hand in Chapter 11 where North–South held:

♠ A Q 5
♥ 10 5
♦ Q J 6 5 3
♣ K 10 5

♠ K 4 3
♥ A K Q 3 2
♦ A 4
♣ A Q 9

South plays in Six No Trumps against the lead of the Jack of Spades. After a ten-minute huddle the declarer surprised the bridgerama audience by playing on Hearts first. Boris observes that after a twenty-minute huddle he couldn't see what prompted South to play on Hearts instead of Diamonds.

I don't say it's right, but I can see the reason quite easily. If you play on Hearts first and find them 4–2 you can decide which way to play the Diamonds. Suppose, for example, the hand is like this:

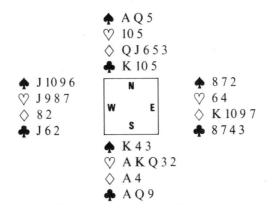

```
                    ♠ A Q 5
                    ♡ 10 5
                    ◇ Q J 6 5 3
                    ♣ K 10 5
   ♠ J 10 9 6          N          ♠ 8 7 2
   ♡ J 9 8 7                       ♡ 6 4
   ◇ 8 2          W       E        ◇ K 10 9 7
   ♣ J 6 2            S            ♣ 8 7 4 3
                    ♠ K 4 3
                    ♡ A K Q 3 2
                    ◇ A 4
                    ♣ A Q 9
```

If you are going to play on Diamonds first it is just as good to play low from hand as to take the simple finesse. As the cards lie above, the Queen of Diamonds loses to the King, and when neither red suit breaks the contract is defeated.

If South begins by playing three rounds of Hearts, on the other hand, he finds that West has the fourth Heart and so takes the Diamond finesse through East. When it wins, he gives up a Heart and makes twelve tricks.

This is not an exhaustive analysis, but I trust it shows that my old friend, Norman Kay, had his reasons.

TERENCE REESE

1
Humour in Bridge

I note that the very first hand I used in my *Sunday Times* column,
when I took over from Kenneth Konstam, was one that would
have amused my old friend enormously; and when Konnie was
amused he laughed loud and long, till everyone had to join in.
This was the hand, from the final of the 1968 Gold Cup.

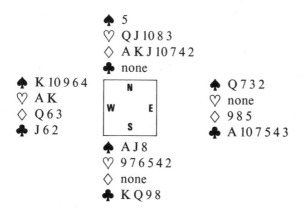

```
              ♠ 5
              ♡ Q J 10 8 3
              ◇ A K J 10 7 4 2
              ♣ none
♠ K 10 9 6 4        N        ♠ Q 7 3 2
♡ A K                        ♡ none
◇ Q 6 3       W       E      ◇ 9 8 5
♣ J 6 2            S         ♣ A 10 7 5 4 3
              ♠ A J 8
              ♡ 9 7 6 5 4 2
              ◇ none
              ♣ K Q 9 8
```

South dealt with both sides vulnerable and at both tables opened
One Heart. I don't disagree with that but the sequel was inevitable.
At one table the bidding went:

South	West	North	East
1 ♡	1 ♠	2 ♠	4 ♠
dble	pass	6 ♡	pass
pass	dble	pass	pass
pass			

When the bid of Six Hearts came round to him, Harrison-Gray,
who was West (and whose team won the event), could not restrain
a slight smile as he took his pipe out of his mouth to double. After
such bidding good players don't double on uncertain tricks in the

side suits, so both North and South guessed their fate before dummy went down.

At the other table the bidding was similar, but when the bid of Six Hearts came round to Jonathan Cansino, West, he passed! You may wonder, if a player can't double a small slam with the Ace and King of trumps, when can he? The answer, after a competitive auction like this, is: only when he has no defensive tricks at all! This (at the time) was a new theory—the "unpenalty double". I don't keep up with all the modern gadgets and this one was news to me, but to be honest I can see the point.

It works like this. When one side has been defending and the other has bid a voluntary slam, a defender with no prospect of a defensive trick doubles, but with one or two tricks he passes. Then the other defender can gauge what to do. With not more than one trick in his own hand he sacrifices; with two tricks he passes the double. If both players gauge the hand right, they will always sacrifice when they can't beat the slam. The only price they pay is that occasionally, as here, a player with two tricks must refrain from doubling. If West had doubled, his partner would have "sacrificed" in Six Spades—and that would have been funnier still.

In retrospect, another difficulty in using the convention comes to mind. If one defender holds, say, Q x in a critical suit, and his partner J x x, neither may regard his holding as a possible trick, even though a loser is inevitable from declarer's point of view. Sometimes, therefore, a pair will "sacrifice" when their opponents have no play for their slam. However, it could be argued that players do this often enough anyhow, whether they are playing the "unpenalty double" or not!

In a rubber-bridge game many years ago my partner and I, holding A K J 9 of trumps between us, suffered the humiliation of winning only one trick in the suit. It may sound unlikely, but the trump set-up was such that the same thing could have happened to anyone. Declarer held 8 x x x x x and dummy Q 10 x. When declarer led a low trump towards dummy my illustrious partner, who held K J 9 and shall be nameless, played the King. I was forced to win the King with the Ace and that was the only trick we got.

I was reminded of this by the deal below when declarer was missing A Q J 9 2 of trumps and still made a slam contract.

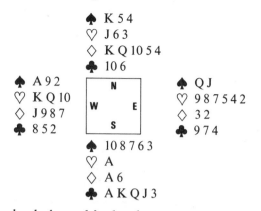

♠ K 5 4
♥ J 6 3
♦ K Q 10 5 4
♣ 10 6

♠ A 9 2   ♠ Q J
♥ K Q 10   ♥ 9 8 7 5 4 2
♦ J 9 8 7   ♦ 3 2
♣ 8 5 2   ♣ 9 7 4

♠ 10 8 7 6 3
♥ A
♦ A 6
♣ A K Q J 3

South was the dealer and both sides were vulnerable. As a result of a bidding sequence too dreadful to publish, South arrived in Six Spades. West led the King of Hearts and South was faced with a seemingly impossible task. But declarer, not one to give up easily, concocted a clever scheme that brought home the bacon. He won the Heart lead with the Ace and cashed the Ace of Diamonds, looking very much like a man with the singleton Ace. Then he led a low trump towards dummy. West could not bear the thought of South getting rid of his (presumed) Heart losers on dummy's K Q of Diamonds, so he climbed up with the Ace and tried to cash the Queen of Hearts. South ruffed and that was the end of the party.

Clearly East should have started a high-low in Diamonds by dropping the three on the first round—then West cannot imagine that he has started with 6 3 2—but this does not detract from South's opportunism.

It is worth mentioning, while on this subject, that there are some standard ways of inducing a crash of honours. Often the technique is to lead a high card from the table towards a weak holding in declarer's hand. This is an example:

J 4
Q 9 7 6 5 3 2

The best chance of losing only one trick is to lead the Jack from dummy. East, with K 10 8, may cover.

Here is another way of putting the defence under pressure:

```
            10 6
   Q                    J 9 8 4
            A K 7 5 3 2
```

Begin by leading the ten from dummy. If East is tempted to cover with the Jack you win and make the next lead from dummy, holding the defence to one trick.

The range of conventions used nowadays often leads to odd and entertaining events. From time to time readers have asked whether it is necessary to learn a lot of systems before playing tournament bridge. Not at all—unknown *systems* are not allowed, and the majority of players still use a Two-Club system. However, a great many *conventions* are played which, in the main, operate in a limited area. I remember a pair at the London Congress—I think they were South Africans—who announced that they played "Two Clubs, with Goldschmidt." They began to explain, but as we were due to play only two boards against them I suggested that they should tell us if this Goldschmidt should happen to occur. On the first hand they missed a game. This was the second:

```
                  ♠ 8 6 4 3 2
                  ♡ 7 6 3
                  ◇ 10
                  ♣ 9 6 5 2
   ♠ A Q 9 5        ┌─────────┐      ♠ 7
   ♡ K 9 2          │    N    │      ♡ J 10 8 5
   ◇ A J 7 4        │ W     E │      ◇ K 8 6 3 2
   ♣ J 8            │    S    │      ♣ A 7 3
                    └─────────┘
                  ♠ K J 10
                  ♡ A Q 4
                  ◇ Q 9 5
                  ♣ K Q 10 4
```

South was the dealer and North–South were vulnerable. The bidding went:

South	West	North	East
1 NT	dble	all pass	

My double with the West hand was far from sound, but in pairs events one has to take chances. It would seem normal for North to remove the double into Two Spades or perhaps, as a preliminary move, into Two Clubs. But perhaps that would have been anti-Goldschmidt.

We began with five tricks in Diamonds and my partner then switched to the Jack of Hearts. The declarer finessed and we cleared the suit. After winning with the Ace of Hearts South exited with a high Club to my partner's Ace. That left the cards as follows with East on lead:

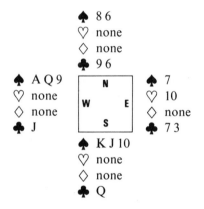

```
               ♠ 8 6
               ♡ none
               ◇ none
               ♣ 9 6
  ♠ A Q 9      ┌─────────┐      ♠ 7
  ♡ none       │    N    │      ♡ 10
  ◇ none       │ W     E │      ◇ none
  ♣ J          │    S    │      ♣ 7 3
               └─────────┘
               ♠ K J 10
               ♡ none
               ◇ none
               ♣ Q
```

The declarer was squeezed on the last Heart. That was six down, for a penalty of 2000. By this time we were being hurried to move on to the next table. We never did discover what Goldschmidt was.

The next two hands could fittingly have come under the heading of "Hands from the Past", but in each case there is an element of humour in the proceedings that makes their inclusion here more appropriate.

The first occurred in a match between leading clubs of Helsinki and Stockholm.

The Finnish North opened with a conventional Two Clubs and his partner responded Two Hearts. This was a positive response, promising an ace and a king. North bid Three Clubs, and South Three Hearts. This (believe it or not) was a transfer bid, asking partner to bid Spades, so that the stronger hand would become the declarer. However, North forgot the system and jumped to

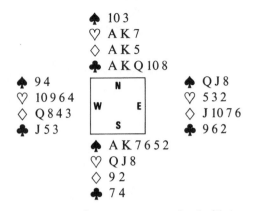

                    ♠ 10 3
                    ♡ A K 7
                    ◇ A K 5
                    ♣ A K Q 10 8
♠ 9 4   ♠ Q J 8
♡ 10 9 6 4   ♡ 5 3 2
◇ Q 8 4 3   ◇ J 10 7 6
♣ J 5 3   ♣ 9 6 2
                    ♠ A K 7 6 5 2
                    ♡ Q J 8
                    ◇ 9 2
                    ♣ 7 4

Seven Hearts. Hoping that partner might hold something like
A K x x in Hearts, South passed. West led a Spade and South
made the first eight tricks with two Spades, three Clubs, two
Diamonds and a Diamond ruff. At trick 9 West had four trumps
left. When South led a Spade, West had to put in the nine of
Hearts to stop dummy's seven from winning. The table over-
ruffed and declarer made the last four tricks on a cross-ruff.

Next, a tall but true story from a non-championship event:

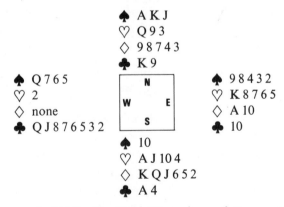

                    ♠ A K J
                    ♡ Q 9 3
                    ◇ 9 8 7 4 3
                    ♣ K 9
♠ Q 7 6 5   ♠ 9 8 4 3 2
♡ 2   ♡ K 8 7 6 5
◇ none   ◇ A 10
♣ Q J 8 7 6 5 3 2   ♣ 10
                    ♠ 10
                    ♡ A J 10 4
                    ◇ K Q J 6 5 2
                    ♣ A 4

Some energetic bidding by East–West threw their opponents off
balance and eventually South contracted for Seven Diamonds.
Before his partner had spoken, East, laughing heartily, doubled
and half-showed his Ace of Diamonds. A joke is a joke, but
equally master points are master points. South summoned the
tournament director, who ruled that the Diamond Ace was an
exposed card and that West was debarred from the auction.

South, no slouch, didn't fancy his prospects in Seven Diamonds with the Ace sitting on the table. He transferred to Seven No Trumps and West led a Spade. You can guess the sequel. At some point in the play South played off two rounds of Clubs and East, still laughing, was obliged to contribute the Ace of Diamonds— playing his exposed card at the first legal opportunity!

Other people's misfortunes have been a source of amusement ever since lame Hephaestus was greeted with Homeric laughter. Two gravity-removing incidents were reported to me in 1970 and, as a result, found their way into my column. The first occurred in golf-club bridge and is best presented from the angle of a defender in the West position who held:

♠ x x
♡ Q J x
◇ A x x x x
♣ A Q x

His partner, at love-all, opened Four Spades, and South over-called with Five Diamonds. West doubled (who wouldn't?) and South removed himself to Six Clubs. West felt impelled to double again and all passed. The contract turned out to be cold, for this was the full deal:

```
               ♠ 10 x x x
               ♡ K x x x x
               ◇ none
               ♣ K 10 x x
  ♠ x x                              ♠ A K Q J x x x
  ♡ Q J x          N                 ♡ 10 x x x
  ◇ A x x x x   W     E              ◇ x x
  ♣ A Q x           S                 ♣ none
               ♠ none
               ♡ A
               ◇ K Q J 10 9 x
               ♣ J 9 x x x x
```

South ruffed the Spade lead and played the nine of Clubs. He let it run when West played low and the rest was easy.

An unlucky double was the feature of this second hand also:

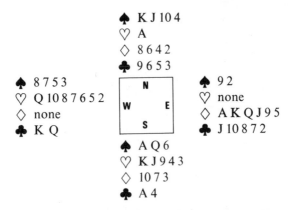

```
              ♠ K J 10 4
              ♡ A
              ◊ 8 6 4 2
              ♣ 9 6 5 3
♠ 8 7 5 3          N          ♠ 9 2
♡ Q 10 8 7 6 5 2             ♡ none
◊ none        W       E      ◊ A K Q J 9 5
♣ K Q              S         ♣ J 10 8 7 2
              ♠ A Q 6
              ♡ K J 9 4 3
              ◊ 10 7 3
              ♣ A 4
```

After East had dealt at game-all, South opened One Heart out of turn. The bidding reverted to East, who opened Four Diamonds. Somewhat flustered, South over-called with Four Hearts. After a decent pause West doubled, and all passed.

West led the King of Clubs to declarer's Ace and a round of Hearts disclosed the 7–0 break. South followed with four rounds of Spades, discarding a Club, and ruffed a Club. With K J 9 of Hearts and 10 7 3 of Diamonds remaining, he exited with a Diamond and made three more trump tricks, thus landing his contract.

Bad bidding makes for strong drama, not to say melodrama. The events described below occurred in the Norwegian Summer Finals, according to a continental magazine that I see from time to time.

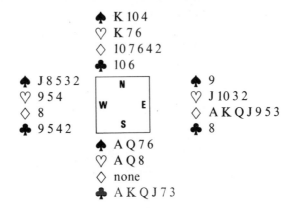

```
              ♠ K 10 4
              ♡ K 7 6
              ◊ 10 7 6 4 2
              ♣ 10 6
♠ J 8 5 3 2        N          ♠ 9
♡ 9 5 4                      ♡ J 10 3 2
◊ 8           W       E      ◊ A K Q J 9 5 3
♣ 9 5 4 2          S         ♣ 8
              ♠ A Q 7 6
              ♡ A Q 8
              ◊ none
              ♣ A K Q J 7 3
```

East was the dealer and North–South were vulnerable. The bidding went as follows:

South	West	North	East
			3 NT (*a*)
6 ♣ (*b*)	6 ♦ (*c*)	dble	pass
6 ♠ (*d*)	pass	pass	pass

No, there are no misprints! Let me interpret: (*a*) East's Three No Trumps was a standard manœuvre, denoting a long, solid minor suit with little strength outside. (*b*) South was an optimist. (*c*) West could tell the sort of hand his partner held, and you may think that he was electing to display his perspicacity when he bid Six Diamonds. But it would be unfair to label him as an exhibitionist: had he passed over Six Clubs he would have been suggesting to his partner that he held some defensive prospects. (*d*) South, bidding Six Spades, was a wild optimist.

West led a Diamond, South ruffed and played off Ace and King of Spades, discovering the 5–1 break. Refusing to despair, he cashed four Clubs, then three rounds of Hearts, finishing in dummy. The cards were now:

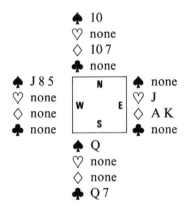

```
                 ♠  10
                 ♡  none
                 ◇  10 7
                 ♣  none
   ♠  J 8 5        ┌─────────┐     ♠  none
   ♡  none         │    N    │     ♡  J
   ◇  none         │ W     E │     ◇  A K
   ♣  none         │    S    │     ♣  none
                 └─────────┘
                 ♠  Q
                 ♡  none
                 ◇  none
                 ♣  Q 7
```

A Diamond was ruffed with the Queen of Spades and poor West could make only one trick. "You did well not to double," South told him gravely.

One of the consoling things about match play, as opposed to rubber bridge, is that, whatever happens at your table, you can always hope that the pair holding your cards in the other room will get an equally poor result. The player from Thailand who held the

West cards on this deal from the 1968 Olympiad was quite philosophic when he lost points in Six Hearts:

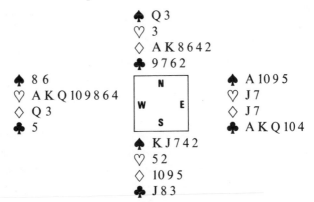

```
            ♠ Q 3
            ♡ 3
            ◇ A K 8 6 4 2
            ♣ 9 7 6 2
♠ 8 6                        ♠ A 10 9 5
♡ A K Q 10 9 8 6 4      N    ♡ J 7
◇ Q 3               W      E  ◇ J 7
♣ 5                      S    ♣ A K Q 10 4
            ♠ K J 7 4 2
            ♡ 5 2
            ◇ 10 9 5
            ♣ J 8 3
```

South was the dealer and East–West were vulnerable. The Lebanese South in the closed room passed, West opened Four Hearts and his partner gave him a direct Six Hearts. North was not greatly troubled to take the first two tricks with the Ace and King of Diamonds.

"Sorry partner," said East. "I thought it was best to bid the slam directly and not tell what to lead."

"Not to worry," said West: "I think it could well be the same at the other table." But it wasn't. I had the full story later from the Lebanese West. This was the bidding:

South	West	North	East
pass	4 ♡	4 NT	dble
5 ♣	pass	pass	dble
pass	pass	pass	

Despite the favourable vulnerability, North's Four No Trumps, asking for a take-out into one of the minor suits, was exceedingly rash. For one thing, players who open with a pre-emptive bid don't always make their contracts.

However, on this occasion East had ample support for his partner. He doubled Four No Trumps and now South made the fatal error of advancing his opinion in front of partner. With three cards of each minor suit, it is clear that he should have passed. When Five Clubs was passed round to East, he doubled after a decent interval.

10

West led the King of Hearts and then made a good switch to a trump. East drew four rounds, on which West discarded one Spade, one Diamond and one Heart. Having drawn the opposing trumps, East led his second Heart.

"The declarer showed no sign of yielding," West related, "so I played off all my Hearts, wondering whether I had miscounted my tricks. We took the last two tricks with the Ace of Spades and a Club, for eleven down. Nothing was said until my partner, in the excitement, wrote down 2200 on his score sheet, attempting to claim honours. This broke the tension and suddenly everyone broke into laughter."

It may be a very old story, but someone reminded me of an incident that caused a great deal of amusement at the time. The occasion was a team-of-eight match between London and another county.

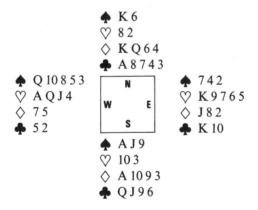

```
              ♠ K 6
              ♡ 8 2
              ◇ K Q 6 4
              ♣ A 8 7 4 3
♠ Q 10 8 5 3    ┌─────┐    ♠ 7 4 2
♡ A Q J 4       │  N  │    ♡ K 9 7 6 5
◇ 7 5         W │     │ E  ◇ J 8 2
♣ 5 2           │  S  │    ♣ K 10
                └─────┘
              ♠ A J 9
              ♡ 10 3
              ◇ A 10 9 3
              ♣ Q J 9 6
```

South dealt at love-all. Normally I don't care for opening One No Trump with an unprotected doubleton, but as South I bid it now and my partner raised to Three No Trumps. West opened with the five of Spades. In an attempt to encourage a Spade continuation by the defence, I went up with the King of Spades and dropped the Jack from hand. Then I crossed to the Ace of Diamonds and ran the Queen of Clubs to East's King. By applying the rule of eleven East was able to see through my jejune effort in the Spade suit. He switched to a low Heart and the defence took five Heart tricks, for two down.

When scores were compared I found that game in No Trumps had been made against one of the London pairs. "Didn't you lead a Heart when you came in with the King of Clubs?" I asked East.

East was the late Guy Ramsey, a bridge journalist who took himself very seriously at the game. "Yes," he said, "I led a Heart and declarer played the ten on it."

"Didn't your partner continue Hearts?" I persisted.

"No," said West. "I rather thought that declarer had the King."

"Perhaps it was partly my fault," said Guy. "Instead of returning my fourth best Heart I led the nine, to silence dummy's eight."

"At my table," I told him, "the eight of hearts didn't make the slightest sound."

Mistakes at bridge usually cost dearly, but sometimes bidding misunderstandings turn out for the best. Who hasn't had his heart wrung by sad tales of opponents stopping in a part-score with 28 or 29 points between them, only to find that no game is on? The hand that follows, however, is rather more of a rarity—the declarer first of all forgot the system and followed by miscounting his tricks. As a result he found himself in an ambitious contract and yet was forced into the only winning line of play.

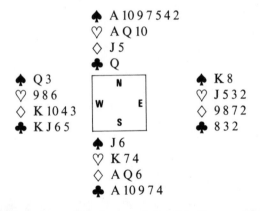

```
                   ♠ A 10 9 7 5 4 2
                   ♡ A Q 10
                   ◇ J 5
                   ♣ Q
  ♠ Q 3                              ♠ K 8
  ♡ 9 8 6             N              ♡ J 5 3 2
  ◇ K 10 4 3     W         E         ◇ 9 8 7 2
  ♣ K J 6 5           S              ♣ 8 3 2
                   ♠ J 6
                   ♡ K 7 4
                   ◇ A Q 6
                   ♣ A 10 9 7 4
```

South dealt at love-all and opened One No Trump. This was the start of the rot—North–South agreed to play strong No Trumps throughout. North forced with Three Spades and South rebid Three No Trumps which North raised to Six No Trumps.

West led the nine of Hearts and declarer considered how to

tackle Spades. If there had been enough entries to the South hand, two finesses would have been best, but instead he won the Heart lead in dummy and followed with Ace and another Spade. When the King and Queen fell together, South, carried away with enthusiasm, claimed the contract and exposed his hand.

East, unimpressed, dourly counted the available tricks and saw that there were only eleven. "Play on, please," he requested. "Remember that you can't take any finesses."

East was quite right. If declarer makes a claim and is required to play on, he is barred from taking any finesses he did not announce at the time of his claim.

There would have been no story if East had played back a Club, but instead he returned a Diamond. With no choice, South won with the Ace, cashed the King and Ace of Hearts, and ran off the Spades. At the end West was squeezed in Diamonds and Clubs and the slam rolled in. Given a free run, South would probably have gone down. The chance of finding the King of Diamonds right was greater than that of finding King of Diamonds, King of Clubs and Jack of Clubs all in one hand—necessary before a squeeze would work.

The events that occurred on the next deal have an air of unreality about them, but I have been assured that the play did indeed follow the course described. The scene was a high-stake game at a London club, so you can imagine the arguments that ensued. These were the four hands:

```
                    ♠ K 6 3 2
                    ♡ Q
                    ◇ K J 4 3
                    ♣ A 8 7 6
   ♠ Q J 10       ┌──────────┐      ♠ A 9 8 7
   ♡ J 4          │    N     │      ♡ 8 5 2
   ◇ Q 9 7 5     W│        E │      ◇ A 10 8
   ♣ K J 9 5      │    S     │      ♣ Q 10 4
                   └──────────┘
                    ♠ 5 4
                    ♡ A K 10 9 7 6 3
                    ◇ 6 2
                    ♣ 3 2
```

North, who as dummy had left the table to make a telephone call (or possibly to express his disapproval of the bidding), was greeted on his return with the news that his partner had made Four Hearts and that the key play had been to ruff a club on the table! Apparently it was impossible.

North dealt at love-all and this was the bidding:

South	West	North	East
		1 ♢	pass
1 ♡	pass	1 ♠	pass
3 ♡	pass	3 NT	pass
4 ♡	pass	pass	pass

The bidding up to Three No Trumps was unexceptionable, but at this point it is clear that North should pass.

West led the Queen of Spades and North made a significant contribution to the course of events when he displayed dummy as follows:

♠ K 6 3 2
♡ none
♢ K Q J 4 3
♣ A 8 7 6

It might be thought that he had mis-sorted his cards deliberately but North denied this strongly. No one noticed anything odd (perhaps he always bid like that!) and the play to the first few tricks proceeded smoothly. Declarer ruffed the third round of Spades and played off A K of Hearts, discarding Clubs from dummy. As the Jack of Hearts had fallen, he continued with the ten for another Club discard and was surprised to find that no one wanted to take the Queen of Hearts. Next came a Diamond to the Jack and Ace and East returned a Diamond. At long last West woke up to the presence of two Queens of Diamonds, but it was too late. The rules are quite clear on this—dummy cannot revoke. All four players are responsible for the correct play of cards from the table. After the rule book had been consulted, play continued with the remaining cards. As you can see, declarer was able to ruff a Club with the newly discovered Queen of Hearts for his tenth trick.

It often seems that team-mates are not sufficiently appreciative

14

at this game. There was the classic story of two Canadian ladies playing in the 1968 Olympiad. They had reached a contract of Six Spades with a combined holding of Q 8 4 3 2 facing A 6 5 and the opponents had started by cashing a side ace. You or I might give up hope, but declarer left trumps alone and started playing a long suit from dummy. Right-hand opponent eventually ruffed with the seven and declarer over-ruffed with the eight. Now all that had to be done was to lead the Queen of Spades from hand and run it (after the second player with K 9 of Spades had failed to cover). Scores were compared. "Minus 450." "Plus 980" (proudly). "Good, we thought you would bid that one!"

A similar but more subtle example came up some years ago in the Gold Cup:

```
              ♠ A K 5
              ♡ 10 4
              ◇ A Q 4 2
              ♣ A K 10 6
♠ 9                             ♠ Q 3 2
♡ J 9 2         ┌─────────┐     ♡ A K Q 7 6 3
◇ K J 10 7 3    │  N      │     ◇ 9 8
♣ J 8 5 2       │ W     E │     ♣ Q 3
                │    S    │
                └─────────┘
              ♠ J 10 8 7 6 4
              ♡ 8 5
              ◇ 6 5
              ♣ 9 7 4
```

East dealt with North–South game and this was the bidding:

South	West	North	East
			1 ♡
pass	2 ♡	dble	4 ♡
pass	pass	dble	pass
4 ♠	pass	pass	pass

West led the two of Hearts and East took the Queen and Ace before switching to the nine of Diamonds. Declarer won in dummy and played off to two Spades to reveal the sure trump loser. Unless West held both the missing Club honours it seemed that there was another loser on the hand, but South decided that he could improve his chances by attempting to squeeze West in the minor suits where it seemed sure that he held length. With that end in mind declarer cashed the Ace of Diamonds and ruffed a Diamond, ensuring that only West could guard the suit. Then came a trump to East's Queen. So far the bidding and play at both tables had been identical, but one East passively played back a Heart at this point. South ruffed and cashed his remaining trumps, squeezing West as planned. At the other table East saw what was coming and made a clever switch to the three of Clubs. Now South could not get off the table without ruffing the last Diamond, thus destroying the menace for a squeeze against West. The only way in which South could make his contract now was by taking an inspired view in the Club suit—in effect playing East for just the holding that he had, and he passed the test by dropping East's Queen.

"So you found the obvious squeeze on hand 19," was the sole commendation from his team-mates!

The Lederer Memorial inter-club contest always seems to produce exciting hands, and, with most of the country's top-ranking pairs taking part, competition is keen. This was one of the more entertaining deals from the 1973 event:

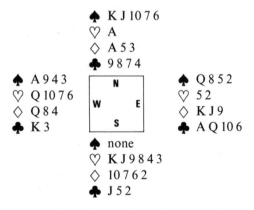

```
                    ♠ K J 10 7 6
                    ♡ A
                    ◇ A 5 3
                    ♣ 9 8 7 4
   ♠ A 9 4 3          ┌─────────┐        ♠ Q 8 5 2
   ♡ Q 10 7 6         │    N    │        ♡ 5 2
   ◇ Q 8 4          W │         │ E      ◇ K J 9
   ♣ K 3              │    S    │        ♣ A Q 10 6
                    └─────────┘
                    ♠ none
                    ♡ K J 9 8 4 3
                    ◇ 10 7 6 2
                    ♣ J 5 2
```

South dealt at love-all and at two tables elected to pass. Where the Regency Club were opposed to the Bridge Academy, one West passed as well and North opened One Spade. After two passes West protected with One No Trump and East bid Two Clubs—a conventional enquiry as to the strength of the No Trump. South joined in with Two Hearts and West doubled to end the auction. He got off to the best lead (as the cards lie) of a low trump and the defenders made no mistakes. As soon as East got the lead he pushed through a second Heart and the declarer was held to five tricks, losing 500 points. This did not look good for the Regency but at the other table their West player opened a mini No Trump (10–12 points). North joined in with Two Spades and was penalised 700 points.

Two South players rated their hand as a Three Heart opening. One was left to play in this contract and escaped for three off to lose 150 points. The other was doubled and the spectators leant forward, expecting a spectacular penalty. However, the West defender chose the disastrous lead of the Ace of Spades. South ruffed, crossed to the Ace of Hearts and took a discard on the King of Spades. Then came the Jack of Spades and East covered with the Queen. At this point South could have settled for eight tricks by ruffing, cashing the King of Hearts and crossing to the Ace of Diamonds in order to throw two more losers on the Spades. Instead South crossed immediately to the Ace of Diamonds to play the ten and seven of Spades. East ruffed and South discarded.

The precise sequence of play that followed is better suppressed —it is sufficient to say that the defenders allowed South another ruff in his own hand and arranged for West to be on lead at trick 12. As a result South made Three Hearts doubled to score 530.

There were fascinating possibilities on the following deal from the

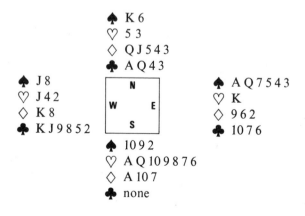

♠ K 6
♡ 5 3
◇ Q J 5 4 3
♣ A Q 4 3

♠ J 8   ♠ A Q 7 5 4 3
♡ J 4 2   ♡ K
◇ K 8   ◇ 9 6 2
♣ K J 9 8 5 2   ♣ 10 7 6

♠ 10 9 2
♡ A Q 10 9 8 7 6
◇ A 10 7
♣ none

1974 Spring Foursomes in a match between two of the fancied teams.

South dealt with East–West vulnerable and at both tables the bidding went:

South	West	North	East
1 ♡	pass	2 ◇	pass
3 ♡	pass	4 ♡	pass
pass	pass		

The play started the same way in both rooms: West led the Jack of Spades to the King, Ace and two; East cashed the Queen of Spades and led a third round of Spades which West ruffed with the Jack of Hearts in front of dummy.

At this point West had a critical decision to make. One player visualized declarer with a holding such as:

♠ 10 9 2
♡ A K Q 10 9 x
◇ A x x
♣ x

and saw that if he passively returned a trump South would simply cash the Ace of Diamonds and run off all the trumps to squeeze him in Diamonds and Clubs. The squeeze had to be broken up, he decided, and at trick 4 he switched to the Jack of Clubs. If the cards lay as West hoped, this would have led to the defeat of the contract, but, as it was, he had given declarer the only chance of making an impossible game. However, South, with no sure entry to the table, elected to win with the Ace of Clubs and finesse in Diamonds. In that way the defenders came to four tricks.

At the other table West played back a trump at trick 4 (the only defence as the cards lie, but losing if the set-up is as visualized by West at the first table). It looked as though declarer's goose was cooked but he gravely played off seven rounds of trumps. West, in the hope of giving declarer a decision to make for his tenth trick, bared his King of Diamonds and saved the K J of Clubs but now South (with no choice) played off the Ace of Diamonds to drop the King. Perhaps the best defence does not always pay. . . .

Reading bridge books is a dangerous hobby for some people. A rubber-bridge partner of mine read an article on deceptive play by declarer. It suggested that with J 9 8 6 5 4 in hand facing K 7 2, the lead of the Jack might gain if a defender covers with Q 10 3— you duck in dummy to bring down the Ace and subsequently finesse the seven to restrict your losers in the suit to one. Very neat, but you can guess what happened when I was dummy on this hand:

♠ K 8 3
♡ A Q J 4
♢ J 5
♣ Q 10 5 2

```
        N
    W       E
        S
```

♠ J 9 7 6 4 2
♡ 9
♢ Q 7
♣ A K J 7

South opened One Spade and, with no opposition bidding, reached Four Spades. West cashed the Ace and King of Diamonds and switched to the two of Hearts. Declarer eyed this suspiciously and decided that he might be helped in the play of the trump suit if he knew which defender held the King of Hearts (remember, East–West had been silent throughout). So he won with dummy's Ace and followed with the Queen of Hearts. East played low in an unconcerned fashion, so South ruffed. It looked as though West had started with A K of Diamonds and King of Hearts. If he had held the Ace of Spades as well he might have bid, and even with a singleton Queen of Spades he might have doubled One Spade. With a glint of triumph in his eye South led the Jack of Spades and, after a moment's thought, West covered with the Queen. Dummy played low and declarer waited expectantly. Alas, this was the complete deal:

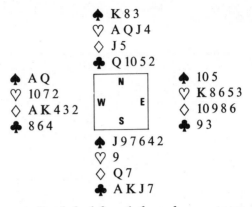

As you can see, South had found the only way to go down.

2
It all Depended on the Bidding . . . .

In top-class bridge, how much depends on bidding? And how much on play? It's an age-old question and one to which no one has attempted to quantify an answer. Looking back over my scrapbook, however, I can see many hands where the bidding was not only critical but influenced the destination of many valued bridge trophies.

Nowadays players have plenty of choice: they can adopt old-fashioned methods (like me); they can play Precision, Blue Club, Roman Club, Neapolitan Club, Livorno Diamond, the list is endless. And many of the systems purport to be tailor-made for slam bidding and the big hands. And yet I still seem to hear the same old post-mortems in which it becomes clear that the system is splendid (whatever it is) but that partner made the wrong bid.

Delving right back to my early days of writing the *Sunday Times* column I find two hands bid on early Acol methods that led to heavy reverses. They both occurred in a practice match played in London against the Venezuelan Olympiad team, and between them cost Britain over 30 international match points.

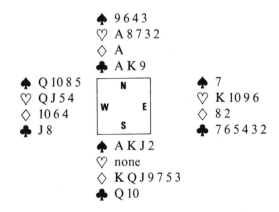

The Venezuelan North–South pair reached Seven Diamonds—
a cast-iron contract, as was Seven No Trumps. For Britain, Mollo
(South) and Gardener were never quite in touch:

South	North
	1 ♡
3 ◇	3 NT
4 ♣	4 NT
6 ◇	pass

North's rebid of Three No Trumps was intended to show a hand
on which he would have rebid Two No Trumps over Two Diamonds. South's Four Club bid was meant to avert a Club lead. If
he fooled anyone, he fooled his partner. Still, I think that North
could have gone seven on the strength of his top cards.

The next hand was a still bigger disaster:

```
                    ♠ K 6 5 4
                    ♡ K 9 6
                    ◇ A K 6
                    ♣ A K 8
   ♠ Q 7 3        ┌──────────┐      ♠ 10 9
   ♡ Q 10 5 2     │    N     │      ♡ J 4 3
   ◇ Q J 8 7 3 2  │ W     E  │      ◇ 10 9 5 4
   ♣ none         │    S     │      ♣ 7 6 5 4
                  └──────────┘
                    ♠ A J 8 2
                    ♡ A 8 7
                    ◇ none
                    ♣ Q J 10 9 3 2
```

South dealt at game to North–South. The Venezuelan South
opened One Spade (One Club was a strong bid on his system)
and sailed into Seven Clubs without opposition. At the other
table:

South (Reese)	West (Rossignol)	North (Flint)	East (Berah)
1 ♣	1 ◇	2 ◇	pass
2 ♠	pass	4 NT	6 ◇ (!)
pass	pass	6 ♠	pass
7 ♠	pass	pass	pass

One down on the Spade finesse. Perhaps North's Four No Trumps was precipitous? Perhaps South should have bid Six Hearts over Six Diamonds? Nobody seemed sure.

Very powerful hands are difficult to express when the opponents get busy. This example was played in the 1960 Olympiad between Italy and one of the American teams. Both players who held the North cards seemed to lose their balance.

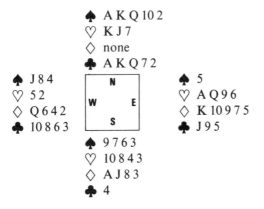

```
                 ♠ A K Q 10 2
                 ♡ K J 7
                 ◇ none
                 ♣ A K Q 7 2
    ♠ J 8 4          N          ♠ 5
    ♡ 5 2                       ♡ A Q 9 6
    ◇ Q 6 4 2      W     E      ◇ K 10 9 7 5
    ♣ 10 8 6 3        S         ♣ J 9 5
                 ♠ 9 7 6 3
                 ♡ 10 8 4 3
                 ◇ A J 8 3
                 ♣ 4
```

East was the dealer and North–South were vulnerable. This was the bidding when the Italians were East–West:

South	West	North	East
			1 ♡ (a)
pass	1 ♠ (b)	pass (c)	2 ◇
pass	pass	3 ◇ (d)	pass
3 ♠	pass	6 ♠ (e)	pass
pass	pass		

(a) At the favourable vulnerability Belladonna makes a sub-minimum opening, relatively safe in the Roman System. (b) West is obliged to respond and this bid of the next suit is artificial and weak. (c) Knowing that East will bid again, North awaits developments. (d) This is the obvious call in a sense, but it is open to the severe disadvantage that partner will probably become declarer. A simple Four Spades, giving up thoughts of a slam, would have turned out better. (e) Now he loses his head a little. There was no reason to assume that Belladonna had made a psychic opening—the Italians almost never do.

West led a Heart and the defenders made the first three tricks for a penalty of 200 points.

The Italians at the other table fared no better. Here the American West opened with a completely psychic Two Clubs and the bidding proceeded:

South	West	North	East
			pass
pass	2 ♣	dble	redble
2 ♡	pass	3 ♣	pass
3 ◇	pass	3 ♠	pass
4 ♠	pass	4 NT	pass
5 ♣	pass	5 NT	pass
6 ♣	pass	6 ♡	pass
pass	pass		

North's Four No Trumps was Blackwood, I think, and the response of Five Clubs showed one ace as they play the convention. It may seem that North was a little over-stimulated by West's psychic opening, but he had an extremely difficult problem. Five Spades is on, but no more with the trumps breaking 3–1. Six Hearts went three down.

There is a situation in bidding where players often show a strange lack of judgement. Suppose you hold an average two-suiter, such as:

♠ A K 10 4 2
♡ 5
◇ A J 8 6 3
♣ Q 5

You open One Spade, the next player over-calls with Two Diamonds, and partner raises to Two Spades. Many players at this point, with some vision, I suppose, of a singleton Diamond and good trumps in dummy, would go straight to Four Spades. But really it is no asset to have your second suit called against you, particularly on your left. No doubt partner is short of Diamonds, but so also is the player on your right, and he will over-ruff the dummy. This is a time for holding back.

You get the same thing on a balanced hand when the player on your left opens, or over-calls, in a suit where you hold something like A K J x or A Q 10 x. Again, it is a bad omen and you should not rush into Three No Trumps just because you have this suit well guarded.

When this freakish hand occurred in rubber bridge, South was an experienced player and did not attempt a slam until his partner had issued two invitations.

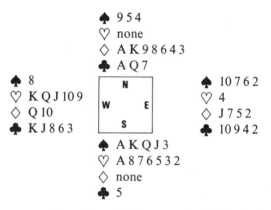

♠ 9 5 4
♡ none
◇ A K 9 8 6 4 3
♣ A Q 7

♠ 8   ♠ 10 7 6 2
♡ K Q J 10 9   N   ♡ 4
◇ Q 10   W   E   ◇ J 7 5 2
♣ K J 8 6 3   S   ♣ 10 9 4 2

♠ A K Q J 3
♡ A 8 7 6 5 3 2
◇ none
♣ 5

Both sides were vulnerable and West was the dealer. West opened One Heart and the bidding continued:

South	West	North	East
	1 ♡	2 ◇	pass
2 ♠	pass	3 ♡	pass
4 ♠	pass	5 ♣	pass
6 ♠	pass	pass	pass

The King of Hearts was led and declarer saw that dummy's trumps were not good enough to allow him to establish the Hearts. Obviously East would be over-ruffing quite early in the proceedings. The Diamond suit offered better prospects, even though dummy seemed to be short of entries.

South ruffed the Heart lead, ruffed a low Diamond in hand, and drew four rounds of trumps. Then he finessed the Queen of Clubs and followed with Ace, King and another Diamond. East won this trick but was forced to return a Club, providing an entry for the remaining Diamonds.

Even in top-level bridge, misunderstandings on the meanings of bids are not uncommon. Some years ago, in the North American Trials, no fewer than three pairs played a lay-down Diamond slam in a part-score, simply because the partnerships concerned had not discussed whether the sequence 1 ◇–1 ♡; 2 NT–3 ◇ was forcing or not. Most players treat this as 100 per cent forcing, but at least three Americans did not!

More recently, and closer to home, a well-known partnership nearly fell out over the interpretation of 1 ♡–1 NT; 2 ◇–3 ♣. The opener maintained that his partner was merely suggesting long Clubs; his partner (with some logic) said that if his Clubs were not worth showing at the two-level they could hardly be worth mentioning at the three-level. His hand, in fact, was x x x of Spades, Q x of Hearts, J 10 x x x of Diamonds and A J x of Clubs; the message that he wanted to convey was that his hand was much improved by his partner's Diamond bid and that he had a control in Clubs. Needless to say, Three Clubs played poorly but Five Diamonds would have had a fair chance.

Mind you, not all misunderstandings end in disaster. Nowadays, if you double an opening bid and, after your partner has responded, bid the opponent's suit, it is accepted that you are showing a strong double and are asking for further information. When the hand below was played, in the 1961 trials, this view was not so widely held.

```
                    ♠ 9 6 3
                    ♡ Q 8 7 3
                    ◇ 8 7 5 4
                    ♣ J 6
    ♠ 8 5                            ♠ K Q J 10 7
    ♡ J 10 6 5 4 2       N           ♡ 9
    ◇ J 9 6          W       E       ◇ K 3 2
    ♣ 9 7                S           ♣ Q 10 8 5
                    ♠ A 4 2
                    ♡ A K
                    ◇ A Q 10
                    ♣ A K 4 3 2
```

With West the dealer at game-all, East opened One Spade after two passes. South doubled and North responded Two Hearts.

Hoping to learn whether his partner's Hearts were long or whether he held a guard in Spades, South forced (as he hoped) with Two Spades. However, North assumed that his partner was attempting to show a Spade suit and passed. A disaster, you think? Not a bit of it! Any game contract by North–South was doomed to fail, and duly did, but in Two Spades South was able to ruff two Clubs on the table and record eight tricks for the only plus score on the North–South cards.

There is something about an adverse Two Club bid that brings out the worst in some players, exciting them into unnatural activity. Usually this ends in disaster, but in the American teams championship, the Vanderbilt Cup, of 1970 Murray seemed to bear a charmed life. On two occasions he intervened in a way that you would not find in any bridge textbook and gained points on both hands.

```
                    ♠ Q 8 6 2
                    ♡ 8
                    ◇ J 10 8 5 4
                    ♣ J 7 6
     ♠ A K                            ♠ 5
     ♡ A K 9 5 3        N             ♡ J 10 4 2
     ◇ A K 7 3       W     E          ◇ 9 6
     ♣ Q 8              S             ♣ A K 9 5 4 2
                    ♠ J 10 9 7 4 3
                    ♡ Q 7 6
                    ◇ Q 2
                    ♣ 10 3
```

With East–West vulnerable West opened Two Clubs and East gave a positive reply of Three Clubs. Undeterred, Murray, as South, came in with Three Spades. West passed and North raised pre-emptively to Five Spades. In spite of this, East–West bid to Seven Clubs. There was no guarantee that they would have made this contract (they would have to find the Queen of Hearts) but perhaps North had seen some of his partner's over-calls before. He decided to take out insurance by bidding Seven Spades. This was doubled and defeated by seven tricks for a gain of 1300 points to East–West, but at the other table they had been allowed (without interference) to play in Six Hearts, scoring 1430 points.

This was Murray's second, and more profitable, venture:

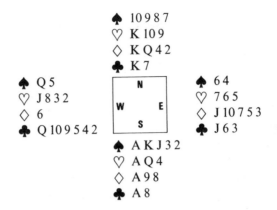

<pre>
              ♠ 10 9 8 7
              ♡ K 10 9
              ◇ K Q 4 2
              ♣ K 7
♠ Q 5   ♠ 6 4
♡ J 8 3 2   N   ♡ 7 6 5
◇ 6   W   E   ◇ J 10 7 5 3
♣ Q 10 9 5 4 2   S   ♣ J 6 3
              ♠ A K J 3 2
              ♡ A Q 4
              ◇ A 9 8
              ♣ A 8
</pre>

South opened Two Clubs at love-all and West (guess who) joined
in with Three Clubs. After that North–South climbed to Seven
Spades with no more interference. However, Murray's over-call
had an effect on the play as South decided to play him for a singleton Spade and took a disastrous second-round finesse in the suit.
At the other table North–South reached the same contract, but
this time South played for the drop in trumps for a big gain.

  Please don't think that I am advocating a policy of lunatic
aggression against Two Clubs—it will not always pay!

In highly competitive situations it usually pays to bid one more
for the road. Accurate defence is more difficult than declarer play,
and if your contract makes, you can set a big gain against a small

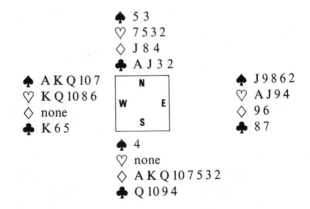

<pre>
              ♠ 5 3
              ♡ 7 5 3 2
              ◇ J 8 4
              ♣ A J 3 2
♠ A K Q 10 7   ♠ J 9 8 6 2
♡ K Q 10 8 6   N   ♡ A J 9 4
◇ none   W   E   ◇ 9 6
♣ K 6 5   S   ♣ 8 7
              ♠ 4
              ♡ none
              ◇ A K Q 10 7 5 3 2
              ♣ Q 10 9 4
</pre>

loss if you have gone too high. The British ladies must have had this advice in mind in the 1961 Olympiad against South Africa. West dealt at game-all and in the open room chose the rather strange-looking opening bid of One Heart. North passed, East raised to Two Hearts and South joined in with an unusual Two No Trumps—true, she had a great many cards in the minor suits, but with 1–0–8–4 distribution it could hardly be said that she was interested in finding out which minor suit partner preferred. Perhaps her aim was to throw the opposition off balance, and in this she certainly succeeded. West bid Four Hearts and after two passes South called Five Diamonds. West pressed on with Five Hearts and North went to Six Diamonds. When this came round to West she judged (rightly) that Six Hearts was not on (11 tricks are the limit with Hearts as trumps) and doubled. With the Club finesse succeeding, South had no trouble in collecting twelve tricks.

At the other table Rixi Markus, as West, rated her hand more highly than her counterpart. This was the bidding:

South	West	North	East
	2 ♣	pass	2 ♡
4 ◇	4 ♠	5 ◇	5 ♠
pass	6 ♠	pass	pass
pass			

East's Two Heart response was Ace-showing and there seemed no reason for West to hold back. After a Diamond lead one of dummy's Clubs went away on the long Heart and the slam rolled in.

If South had decided not to save in Seven Diamonds I think she should have doubled the final contract—a Lightner slam double, suggesting that Six Spades may be defeated on an unusual lead. Whether North would have found the killing Heart lead is debatable, but she would have been warned against her actual Diamond opening. A Heart lead would have led to a two-trick defeat.

Almost immediately after writing up the above hand, my attention was drawn to another highly competitive deal from match play where the same advice to bid on would have succeeded. In the event one team gained by sacrificing at one table and approaching their slam in a roundabout way at the other.

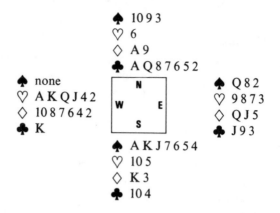

```
                    ♠ 10 9 3
                    ♡ 6
                    ◇ A 9
                    ♣ A Q 8 7 6 5 2
♠ none                  N              ♠ Q 8 2
♡ A K Q J 4 2      W         E         ♡ 9 8 7 3
◇ 10 8 7 6 4 2                         ◇ Q J 5
♣ K                     S              ♣ J 9 3
                    ♠ A K J 7 6 5 4
                    ♡ 10 5
                    ◇ K 3
                    ♣ 10 4
```

South dealt at game-all and at one table opened Four Spades.
West joined in with Five Hearts and North, hoping for the best,
plunged to Six Spades. After two passes West decided that as his
opponents had bid with such confidence a sacrifice was in order.
He went on to Seven Diamonds, East put him back to Seven Hearts,
and this was doubled. There was nothing in the play and declarer
lost the obvious three tricks to concede 800 points.

There were several surprising features to the auction in the
other room:

South	West	North	East
1 ♠	2 ♡	3 ♣	pass
3 ♠	pass	4 ♠	pass
pass	5 ◇	pass	5 ♡
5 ♠	pass	6 ♠	pass
pass	pass		

To start with, West had an awkward hand to bid over One Spade.
Two Hearts, Three Hearts and Four Hearts would all have their
supporters, and neither a double nor an over-call of Two Spades
would be too outrageous. On the next round he could be sure of
some more bidding and decided to wait until the opponents had
exhausted themselves. When Four Spades was passed round to
him it seemed that this moment had come, but after his injudi-
cious re-opening of Five Diamonds, North–South found a new lease
on life! At the end both East and West were left with a nightmare
decision—from the way that North–South had conducted their

operations there was no certainty that Six Spades would make. Again there were no problems in the play and with the Queen of Spades and King of Clubs co-operating, twelve tricks rolled in for a score of 1430 points. It is easy to be wise after the event, but how would you have coped with these hands if they had cropped up in your weekly duplicate?

Another possibility in the field of competitive bidding is the advance sacrifice—an idea that appeals to some players. In theory, the concept of rushing the bidding and forcing the opponents to miss their best contract is an attractive one. Sometimes it works well, but not always. Here are two examples from match play:

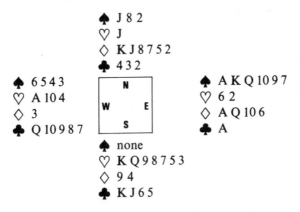

```
                    ♠ J 8 2
                    ♡ J
                    ◇ K J 8 7 5 2
                    ♣ 4 3 2
    ♠ 6 5 4 3         ┌─────────┐         ♠ A K Q 10 9 7
    ♡ A 10 4          │    N    │         ♡ 6 2
    ◇ 3           W   │         │   E     ◇ A Q 10 6
    ♣ Q 10 9 8 7      │    S    │         ♣ A
                      └─────────┘
                    ♠ none
                    ♡ K Q 9 8 7 5 3
                    ◇ 9 4
                    ♣ K J 6 5
```

At one table East opened Two Spades and, although South joined in with Four Hearts, West bid Five Hearts and his partner needed no more encouragement. There were no problems in the play in Six Spades.

At the other table East chose to open Two Clubs and South seized his chance, not being vulnerable, by bidding Five Hearts. West could do no more than double and there was little that East could do. The defence took the maximum: West led the three of Diamonds to the Queen, and East cashed the Ace of Clubs before returning the six of Diamonds. West ruffed, East ruffed the Club return and played another Diamond. South ruffed high, but West over-ruffed and gave his partner a second Club ruff. Now came a fourth Diamond and it is only charitable to assume that South had miscounted trumps for he trumped with the nine of Hearts and lost yet one more trick. The defenders made all five of their trumps, but that was only 900 points compared with the 1430 gained at the other table.

That sacrifice paid off, but this one did not:

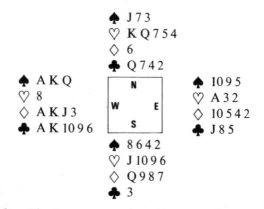

```
              ♠ J 7 3
              ♡ K Q 7 5 4
              ◇ 6
              ♣ Q 7 4 2
♠ A K Q           N          ♠ 10 9 5
♡ 8                          ♡ A 3 2
◇ A K J 3    W        E       ◇ 10 5 4 2
♣ A K 10 9 6       S         ♣ J 8 5
              ♠ 8 6 4 2
              ♡ J 10 9 6
              ◇ Q 9 8 7
              ♣ 3
```

West dealt with East–West vulnerable and opened Two Clubs. North intervened with Two Hearts and, after a pass by East, South raised to Five Hearts. This went round to East who doubled. You can see what happened—East–West collected 700 points, but it was the only plus score recorded on their cards. Elsewhere, their hands had been played in Six Clubs, Six Diamonds, or Three No Trumps and these contracts had failed by one or two tricks. There must be a moral here somewhere—perhaps it is just that you should not sacrifice unless your opponents *can* make something!

3
No Swing

When the records of a match show that there has been no swing (i.e. the same score has been achieved in both rooms) on a hand, commentators tend to skip on and look for something more exciting. This deal was just such a "flat board" from the 1959 Gold Cup.

```
              ♠ 8 4
              ♡ Q J 9 3 2
              ◇ A J 6 3
              ♣ 7 5
  ♠ K 10 2         N          ♠ J 9 7 6 5
  ♡ 8 5                       ♡ A 10 4
  ◇ 9 5 4 2    W       E      ◇ Q 7
  ♣ K J 9 2                   ♣ 10 6 3
                   S
              ♠ A Q 3
              ♡ K 7 6
              ◇ K 10 8
              ♣ A Q 8 4
```

East dealt with North–South Vulnerable. At my table, looking for points, I chose to open the East hand with One No Trump and the auction unfolded as follows:

South	West	North	East
			1 NT
dble	pass	4 ♡	pass
4 NT	pass	5 ◇	pass
5 ♡	pass	pass	pass

As often happens, once North–South suspected that they were being talked out of something they got too high before they could put the brakes on. I led a low Spade and the Queen lost to the King. There was no escaping the loss of a trick in both trumps and Clubs, and when finally declarer mis-guessed the Diamonds to go two off, I felt convinced that my team had gained handsomely.

It wasn't to be, however, for at the other table my team-mate in the South seat became declarer in Three No Trumps after an uncontested auction. West led the eight of Hearts (it didn't look a particularly punishing attack!) and dummy's nine was allowed to win. Declarer continued Hearts and East took his Ace and switched to the nine of Spades—a good shot, better than a low Spade which would have let declarer play low from hand and keep his A Q of Spades protected. South put in the Queen of Spades only to lose to the King and the defenders cleared the Spades. There would have been no story if declarer had guessed the Diamond position, but the lead of the nine of Spades had a dual effect —South now placed West with the length in Spades. As a result he took the Diamond finesse into what he thought was the safe hand, going two down to duplicate the result at the other table.

In retrospect it is easy to see how South should have played the hand. Once the nine of Hearts has held the first trick he should lead a low Diamond from the table and finesse the ten of Diamonds. Win or lose, he has at least three Diamond tricks and West cannot profitably lead either black suit. As a result, South has plenty of time to establish the Hearts and make his contract.

After the above hand appeared, several readers were prompted to write in to describe similar deals. One letter reminded me of a celebrated hand from a Lederer Memorial match. John Collings's team-mates returned to the table well satisfied with having played in Four Spades doubled with an overtrick to score 990 points.

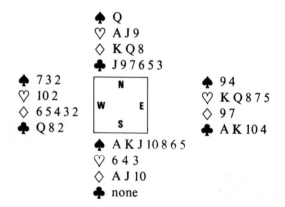

"No swing," observed John, "we lost 1000 in Three No Trumps redoubled the other way!"

The hands on the opposite page provide another example.

North dealt at game-all and opened One Club. East over-called with One Heart and eventually South played in Six Spades against which West led the ten of Hearts. There was no future in going in with the Ace, so declarer covered with dummy's Jack and East won with the Queen.

So far the play at both tables had been identical, but now one East tried to cash the Ace of Clubs. South ruffed and there were enough entries to the table to establish a Club for the twelfth trick.

At the other table East correctly judged that declarer was void in Clubs and at trick 2 he returned a Diamond. Without the benefit of a Club lead South was now an entry short to establish dummy's long suit. However, he won with the Ace of Diamonds, crossed to the Queen of Spades and ruffed a Club. Then he drew trumps, used the Queen of Diamonds to ruff another Club, and played off some more trumps to reach this position:

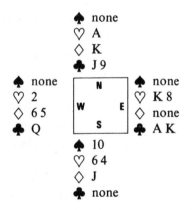

```
              ♠ none
              ♡ A
              ◇ K
              ♣ J 9
   ♠ none      ┌─────────┐    ♠ none
   ♡ 2         │    N    │    ♡ K 8
   ◇ 6 5       │ W     E │    ◇ none
   ♣ Q         │    S    │    ♣ A K
              └─────────┘
              ♠ 10
              ♡ 6 4
              ◇ J
              ♣ none
```

Declarer crossed to the King of Diamonds and East was finished—caught in a trump squeeze. A Heart discard would give South the rest of the tricks, and to part with a Club would allow dummy's Jack to be established with a ruff.

The Lederer Memorial provided another good "no swing" deal. This time the year was 1960 and the cards lay as follows:

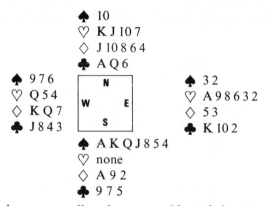

```
                    ♠ 10
                    ♡ K J 10 7
                    ◇ J 10 8 6 4
                    ♣ A Q 6
    ♠ 9 7 6          ┌─────────┐         ♠ 3 2
    ♡ Q 5 4          │    N    │         ♡ A 9 8 6 3 2
    ◇ K Q 7          │ W     E │         ◇ 5 3
    ♣ J 8 4 3        │    S    │         ♣ K 10 2
                     └─────────┘
                    ♠ A K Q J 8 5 4
                    ♡ none
                    ◇ A 9 2
                    ♣ 9 7 5
```

South dealt at game-all and at one table ended in Four Spades.
West led the three of Clubs and you can see how the play developed: dummy played low and East won with the ten. A Diamond
came back and West was allowed to score his Queen. Now another
Club finished declarer's chances as there was no way of avoiding
the loss of one more trick in each minor suit. Not unnaturally,
West felt pleased with his opening lead. Had he chosen anything
other than a Club, South would have had ample time to come to
ten tricks.

When the time came for comparison West's only thought was
to ask what had been the opening lead at the other table. On
hearing that it was the King of Diamonds he was confident of a
substantial gain. However, the demeanour of his team-mates suggested that all was not well. Investigation revealed that they had
wound their way to Seven Spades and that the lead had enabled
them to escape for one off to tie the board.

Wild horses would not drag from me the identity of the North–
South pair concerned. The rot had started when South opened
Two Spades—although he held eight playing tricks, the hand is
somewhat empty for a two-bid—and continued when North responded Three Diamonds. South then supported Diamonds and
the partners assured each other that they did hold all the necessary controls. Unfortunately, there were gaps in the Diamond
suit; it may well be that North was ill-advised to give a positive
response with such a poor suit. Incidentally, West's lead of the
King of Diamonds struck me as curious—you don't usually try
to *establish* tricks when defending against a grand slam.

A rather more academic "no swing" hand came up in the 1962 European Championship in Beirut. The hand was a good argument in favour of those players who maintain that no four-card major suit is too weak to bid, for even a trump suit of 10 x x x facing J x x x is playable at the game level, so long as the remaining values are sufficient.

This is the deal, from the Britain *v.* France match:

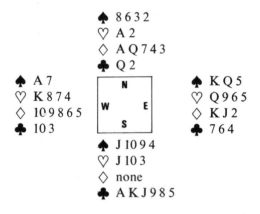

North was the dealer at game-all. Swinnerton-Dyer and Barbour, for Britain, sailed into Four Spades and West led a Heart. The declarer went up with the Ace and played three rounds of Clubs, intending to dispose of dummy's Heart loser; but when West ruffed with the Seven of Spades he over-ruffed, came back to hand with a Diamond ruff, and led a fourth Club in this position:

♠ 6 3 2
♡ 2
◇ A Q 7 4
♣ none

♠ A   ♠ K Q 5
♡ K 8 7   ♡ Q 9 5
◇ 10 9 8 6   ◇ K 2
♣ none   ♣ none

♠ J 10 9
♡ J 10
◇ none
♣ K 9 8

West ruffed with the Ace of Spades (best defence) and dummy's Heart went away. West exited with a Diamond and South ruffed. After a Heart ruff the Ace of Diamonds dropped the King, and the Queen of Diamonds was ruffed high by East. A high Spade was cashed, but declarer had to win the last two tricks. Alas for the hopes of a British gain, for as it turned out the French pair had reached the same contract and made it by a similar sequence of play.

When opponents are presented with a game at both tables in the European Championship, it is fair to assume that the hand contains some points of interest. The following deal occurred in Britain's opening match against Norway in 1971 and although the purist might complain that, strictly speaking, it was not a "no swing" deal the final difference between the two scores was very small.

```
                    ♠ Q J 9 6 3
                    ♡ K 4 3
                    ◇ Q 8 6 4
                    ♣ 9
    ♠ A 10 5         ┌──────────┐      ♠ K 8 7
    ♡ 6 5            │    N     │      ♡ Q 10
    ◇ A 9 7          │  W   E   │      ◇ 10 3 2
    ♣ Q J 10 6 2     │    S     │      ♣ A K 8 4 3
                    └──────────┘
                    ♠ 4 2
                    ♡ A J 9 8 7 2
                    ◇ K J 5
                    ♣ 7 5
```

East was the dealer and neither side was vulnerable. This was the bidding when Britain was North–South:

South	West	North	East
			1 NT
2 ♡	2 NT	4 ♡	pass
pass	dble	pass	pass
pass			

North's raise to Four Hearts strikes me as a bit of a flyer, but the venture was successful. West led the Queen of Clubs and switched to a trump, won by the Ace. The declarer, Robert Sheehan, ruffed his second Club, then led a Diamond from the table and put on the King. West won and played his second trump, allowing declarer to discard a Spade on the thirteenth Diamond. West's misjudgement of the situation was understandable, but there were several reasons for placing his partner with the King of Spades.

At the other table the East–West performance was even less impressive. The bidding went:

South	West	North	East
			1 NT
2 ♡	2 NT	3 ♡	pass
pass	dble	pass	pass
pass			

West's double ("Partner has opened One No Trump and I have eleven points, so how can they make Three Hearts?") is, I always think, one of the silliest ways of giving away points. He led a trump and then a second trump when in with the Ace of Diamonds, so again South made ten tricks, scoring 630 points against the 590 points conceded at the other table. Despite their misadventure at the first table, the Norwegians gained a match point, but both North–South pairs must have been disappointed to find that their side had not done better.

Although the next hand, like the last, led to a small gain to one side, I have been tempted to include it under the "no swing" umbrella, for again both declarers had every reason to suppose they had gained comfortably over their counterparts.

```
                    ♠ K 9 8 7
                    ♡ 6 4 2
                    ◇ 10 5
                    ♣ A 10 9 6
   ♠ 6 4            ┌──────────┐      ♠ 3 2
   ♡ K 10 5 3       │    N     │      ♡ J 9 8
   ◇ K Q J 7 6 4    │ W     E  │      ◇ A 9 8 3 2
   ♣ 2              │    S     │      ♣ Q 5 3
                    └──────────┘
                    ♠ A Q J 10 5
                    ♡ A Q 7
                    ◇ none
                    ♣ K J 8 7 4
```

South dealt at game-all and at one table chose to open One Spade. After some interference by East–West in Diamonds, South ended in Six Spades and West led the King of Diamonds. The hand looked simple enough; if declarer could locate the Queen of Clubs or find the Heart finesse right there would be no problem, but South read a little more into the situation. He saw that if he could eliminate Diamonds and draw trumps it might not matter if he misguessed the Clubs. With this idea in mind he ruffed high in hand, crossed to the seven of Spades, and ruffed the last Diamond. A Spade to the King cleared the trumps and South continued with the Ace and ten of Clubs, which he let run. He did not mind if West held the doubleton Queen for then he would be end-played and there would be no need for the Heart finesse. However, the ten won and South had twelve tricks.

At the other table South preferred One Club for his opening bid. As a result the contract this time was Six Clubs. Again West led the King of Diamonds and South considered his problem. There were the same basic chances for Six Clubs as there were for Six Spades, but it looked as though there was no chance of an end-play unless Spades could be eliminated before touching trumps. Nevertheless, South decided to try his luck. First he had to cash two Spade tricks. To reduce the chances of a ruff in case East held a singleton Spade, declarer led the Jack of Spades to dummy's King and returned the Nine of Spades. He reasoned that if East held Q x x of Clubs he might be reluctant to ruff what looked like a loser. However, all went peacefully and South was able to ruff dummy's second Diamond. Then the Ace of Clubs followed by the ten assured the contract as at the other table. As South was heard to remark afterwards, it had seemed an awful lot of work to lose 2 international match points, for he had scored only 1370 points compared with the 1430 at the other table.

As I have cheated slightly with the last two examples, I will finish with another genuine "no swing" deal. It is always difficult to decide on the best action to take when an opponent bids a suit in which you are strong, and this was no exception. By passing on a strong hand you may gain by collecting a penalty with no game likely for your side; but equally you may lose points if a game is available and the penalty is not enough to compensate. On the following hand, a happy balance was struck. . . .

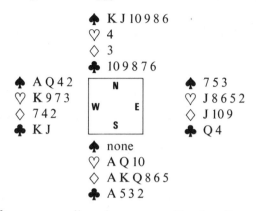

```
              ♠ K J 10 9 8 6
              ♡ 4
              ◇ 3
              ♣ 10 9 8 7 6
♠ A Q 4 2          N          ♠ 7 5 3
♡ K 9 7 3      W       E      ♡ J 8 6 5 2
◇ 7 4 2                       ◇ J 10 9
♣ K J             S          ♣ Q 4
              ♠ none
              ♡ A Q 10
              ◇ A K Q 8 6 5
              ♣ A 5 3 2
```

West dealt at game-all and at one table, handicapped by his system which included five-card majors and a strong No Trump, chose to open One Diamond. This was passed round to South who decided to take whatever was available by passing rather than pressing for a problematical game. West's odd-looking contract went six down to give North–South 600 points. (North led his singleton Heart, took a ruff, and played a Club. South won, drew trumps, and cleared the Clubs. Badly rattled West tried to cash the Ace of Spades instead of the King of Hearts, which he knew would win, and as a result went down one more than was necessary.)

At the other table West made a more natural opening bid and South ended in Five Diamonds. He made eleven tricks to score 600 points, exactly duplicating the score at the first table.

4
Is there <u>any</u> Chance?

From both declarer's and the defenders' points of view you often get hands where it is clear that orthodox play will get you precisely nowhere. If you are lost anyhow, a departure from normality can hardly cost much and will, on happy occasions, persuade the other side to go wrong. This deal is a good example—I think you will admire East's play:

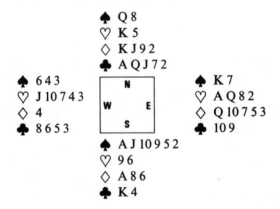

West was the dealer and East–West were vulnerable. The bidding went:

South	West	North	East
	pass	1 ♣	pass
1 ♠	pass	1 NT	pass
3 ♠	pass	4 ♠	pass
pass	pass		

West led the four of Diamonds and dummy played low. With the two and three in sight, East could read his partner for a singleton Diamond. Even so, defensive prospects looked poor. If South held two aces, as was likely, he might easily make thirteen tricks. There was just one chance—that South could be deflected from the trump finesse. When dummy played a low Diamond on the first trick, East played the Queen! The declarer now thought to himself: "That Queen of Diamonds might be a singleton. If I take the finesse in Spades they may make two Heart tricks, followed by a Diamond ruff. It must be safer to play Ace of Spades and another." This plan failed sadly. East won the second Spade and gave his partner a Diamond ruff. Then a Heart through the King defeated the contract. South ended up with nine tricks instead of thirteen. Opportunities for this type of defence are quite common. Just pretend that you have a singleton and you may prevent declarer from taking a winning finesse in the trump suit.

Some years ago Eric Jannersten showed me a hand from the Swedish pairs championship:

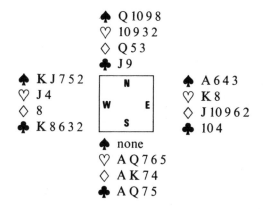

South dealt with North–South vulnerable. This was the bidding:

South	West	North	East
1 ♡	1 ♠	2 ♡	2 ♠
4 ♡	4 ♠	dble	pass
5 ♡	pass	pass	pass

"I would have been happy to defend against Four Spades doubled," I remarked. "That looks like 700 at least."

"Maybe," said Eric. "But you are in Five Hearts, and the question is can you see any way in which the contract might be beaten after a Spade lead?"

"I can see that if you make the safety play in Hearts, laying down the Ace first, you might make only five," I said. "But to go down? Suppose you ruffed the Spade, cashed Ace of Hearts, and crossed to dummy with the Queen of Diamonds. Instead of playing a second round of trumps you lead the Jack of Clubs. West holds off, wins the next round with the King, gives his partner a ruff, and ruffs the Diamond return. That would do it. I've seen worse."

"But declarer finessed the Queen of Hearts, and he didn't play all that badly," said Eric.

I saw the point then, and I won't keep the reader in suspense. After ruffing the Ace of Spades South entered dummy with a Diamond and led the nine of Clubs to the Queen and King. West returned a Club to dummy's Jack, and South finessed the Queen of Hearts. On this trick West dropped the Jack of Hearts, a simple but devastating false card. Thinking that he had to pick up East's K x, South led a third Club, ruffed with the nine and got over-ruffed. Now a Diamond from East allowed West to make his four of Hearts.

Oddly enough, the same card featured in an almost identical defence found by Jonathan Cansino when I played with him in the 1971 Juan-les-Pins Bridge Festival. This was the layout then:

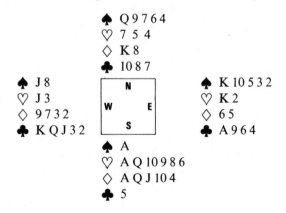

♠ Q 9 7 6 4
♡ 7 5 4
◇ K 8
♣ 10 8 7

♠ J 8
♡ J 3
◇ 9 7 3 2
♣ K Q J 3 2

♠ K 10 5 3 2
♡ K 2
◇ 6 5
♣ A 9 6 4

♠ A
♡ A Q 10 9 8 6
◇ A Q J 10 4
♣ 5

At game-all South opened Two Hearts and ended in an optimistic Six Hearts. West led the King of Clubs and declarer ruffed the second round. He crossed to the King of Diamonds and, after some thought, finessed the Queen of Hearts. It was clear that he

44

had done the right thing, so Jonathan dropped the Jack of Hearts under the Queen—a play that could hardly cost. Placing East with both remaining Hearts, South attempted to reach dummy with a Diamond ruff and now East scored the King of Hearts.

Again from Juan-les-Pins, but a year later, came this opportunity for fine play, this time by declarer. Imagine that you pick up the following collection:

♠ A K Q J 2
♡ none
♢ A K 9 3
♣ A K Q 4

Having checked anxiously that you hold the right number of cards, you open Two Clubs. The player on your left over-calls with Four Hearts and your partner doubles. What now?

The sequence occurred at several tables. Most Souths pressed on with Five Hearts, determined to reach a slam in some department. North bid Six Clubs which proved impossible after a Heart lead. This was the full hand:

```
                 ♠ 10 6 5
                 ♡ Q 9 7
                 ♢ 10 5 4
                 ♣ 10 5 3 2
  ♠ 7 4 3              N            ♠ 9 8
  ♡ A J 10 8 6 5 4 3        W   E   ♡ K 2
  ♢ 2                               ♢ Q J 8 7 6
  ♣ 6                  S            ♣ J 9 8 7
                 ♠ A K Q J 2
                 ♡ none
                 ♢ A K 9 3
                 ♣ A K Q 4
```

South was the dealer with neither side vulnerable. At some tables the bidding went:

South	West	North	East
2 ♣	4 ♡	dble	pass
6 ♠	pass	pass	pass

Clearly this was something of a risk by South, but one player actually made his contract after West had made the ill-judged lead of the Ace of Hearts. Declarer ruffed high, entered dummy with the Ten of Spades on the third round of trumps, and ruffed another Heart, bringing down East's King. Then came the Ace and King of Clubs, followed by the nine of Diamonds. If East takes the trick he must give dummy the lead and the Queen of Hearts provides a discard. If East lets the nine of Diamonds hold, South end-plays him in Diamonds and Clubs. The hand is more or less a double-dummy problem when West leads the Ace of Hearts and follows to three rounds of Spades, but it was still a very fine achievement at the table.

Anyone who simply took all the available finesses on the next deal would fare badly, but the declarer at the table was able to deduce from the bidding how the missing high cards were divided, and also spotted how to take advantage of this knowledge.

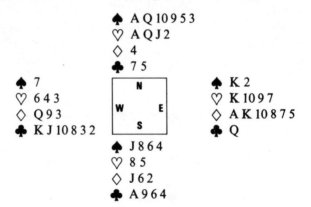

♠ A Q 10 9 5 3
♡ A Q J 2
♢ 4
♣ 7 5

♠ 7
♡ 6 4 3
♢ Q 9 3
♣ K J 10 8 3 2

♠ K 2
♡ K 10 9 7
♢ A K 10 8 7 5
♣ Q

♠ J 8 6 4
♡ 8 5
♢ J 6 2
♣ A 9 6 4

At love-all the bidding went:

South	West	North	East
			1 ♢
pass	2 ♣	dble	2 ♡
2 ♠	pass	4 ♠	pass
pass	pass		

West led the three of Diamonds; East won with the King and switched to his singleton Queen of Clubs. From the bidding and

46

the first two plays it became evident to South (1) that West had
Q x x of Diamonds and six Clubs to the K J 10, and (2) that
East, for his free bid of Two Hearts, must hold both major suit
kings as well as a good suit of Diamonds. Abandoning hope of a
successful finesse in either major suit, South won the Club, ruffed
a Diamond and played off Ace and another Spade. East won with
the King and returned the Ace of Diamonds, expecting dummy to
ruff. But instead of ruffing declarer discarded dummy's second
Club, and now East was at the end of his rope. He had either to
lead a Heart into the A Q or concede a ruff and discard.

It is true that East could have escaped the trap by returning
a low Diamond instead of the Ace at trick 6, but are you quite
sure that *you* would have seen the danger in time?

Here is another one to test your powers of imagination as
declarer:

```
                    ♠ 9 8 5 3
                    ♡ A Q 4 2
                    ◇ 6 2
                    ♣ A 9 4
      ♠ 10 6                           ♠ A 4
      ♡ K 10 8           N             ♡ 9 7 5
      ◇ A 3         W         E        ◇ 10 9 8 7 5 4
      ♣ K J 10 8 6 2        S          ♣ 7 5
                    ♠ K Q J 7 2
                    ♡ J 6 3
                    ◇ K Q J
                    ♣ Q 3
```

With North the dealer and both sides vulnerable the bidding
goes:

South	West	North	East
		pass	pass
1 ♠	2 ♣	3 ♠	pass
4 ♠	pass	pass	pass

West begins with Ace and another Diamond. East wins the first
round of trumps and plays a third Diamond, which West ruffs
with the ten of Spades.

Which of your pearls are you going to discard from dummy? As you have lost three tricks already it may seem that dummy's fourth Heart is not particularly valuable, and the four of Clubs is not going to win a trick either. Nevertheless, you cannot afford to part with either the two of Hearts or the four of Clubs; you must play a trump from dummy under West's ten of Spades!

Now it's clear that West must not lead a Heart, as that would give you four Heart tricks. West exits with the King of Clubs, therefore. This gives you one trick and it is not hard to see where the other will come from. You draw the outstanding trump, finesse the Queen of Hearts, return to the Queen of Clubs, and run down the trumps. Playing in front of dummy, West is squeezed in Hearts and Clubs.

In most cases it's not difficult to establish what the par result of a deal should be. You look at the four hands, assume normally good bidding and play, and the outcome is called par. But, as in golf, a player should break par once in a while. An unusual set of circumstances may give him an opportunity to upset all advance calculations. Consider the deal below, played by South in Three No-Trumps against a Heart lead. It looks as though par for the course is ten tricks, thanks to the fortunate lie of the Spades. Indeed, South can make eleven tricks if he reads the hand perfectly and end-plays East, forcing him to lead into dummy's Diamonds. Nevertheless, West managed to create a diversion, and instead of the routine ten tricks, South had only eight.

```
                    ♠ Q 9 8 5 4
                    ♡ A 2
                    ◇ A K J
                    ♣ 8 6 5
  ♠ K J 10          ┌─────────┐      ♠ 7 6 3
  ♡ Q 8 7 6 5 3     │    N    │      ♡ J 10
  ◇ 7 5             │ W     E │      ◇ Q 10 3 2
  ♣ J 4             │    S    │      ♣ Q 10 9 2
                    └─────────┘
                    ♠ A 2
                    ♡ K 9 4
                    ◇ 9 8 6 4
                    ♣ A K 7 3
```

South was dealer at game-all and the bidding went:

South	West	North	East
1 ♣	pass	1 ♠	pass
1 NT	pass	3 NT	pass
pass	pass		

West led the six of Hearts and declarer could see seven top winners. There was something to be said for ducking the first round of Hearts, but it might have been a mistake to allow the opponents to switch to Clubs with a Heart in the bag, so South won with the Ace of Hearts and led a Spade to the Ace. Observing the sinister lie of the Spade suit, West dropped the King, in order to give South the impression that J 10 7 6 3 were stacked in the East hand.

An experienced declarer, playing against an equally experienced defender, would have continued Spades with a pitying look, but South now turned to Diamonds for his ninth trick, finessing the Jack. East won and led his second Heart, West over-taking with his Queen to clear the suit. When the Diamonds brought no joy, South cashed the Ace and King of Clubs, then led a low Spade, thinking that East was down to J 10 x x of Spades. Alas for the intended throw-in, West was bound to gain the lead in Spades and had enough winners to set the contract.

Luck in bridge takes many forms, but the better a player is the luckier he seems to be. This may be because in a seemingly hopeless contract he can spot unlikely chances that a lesser player would overlook altogether. I can remember, many years ago, watching West on the deal below playing in an appalling contract of Seven No-Trumps against the lead of the Queen of Diamonds.

West	East
♠ 10	♠ A K J 7 6
♡ A K 7 4 3	♡ 5 2
◇ A K 6 5	◇ 4 3 2
♣ A K 5	♣ Q 7 6

After inspecting dummy West flamboyantly announced success if North held precisely Q 9 8 in Spades and either defender held four or more cards in both red suits. And they had!—but I shall leave you to work out the play.

A more recent but not much more hopeful slam was the following:

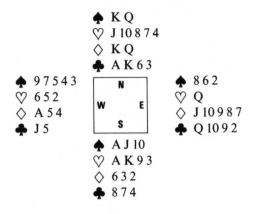

```
                      ♠ K Q
                      ♡ J 10 8 7 4
                      ◇ K Q
                      ♣ A K 6 3
   ♠ 9 7 5 4 3         N           ♠ 8 6 2
   ♡ 6 5 2        W         E      ♡ Q
   ◇ A 5 4             S           ◇ J 10 9 8 7
   ♣ J 5                           ♣ Q 10 9 2
                      ♠ A J 10
                      ♡ A K 9 3
                      ◇ 6 3 2
                      ♣ 8 7 4
```

South chose to open One No-Trump and, after a Stayman enquiry by North, ended in Six Hearts. West led a trump to solve one of declarer's problems, but it still looked impossible to avoid the loss of a trick in each minor suit. However, South saw a slight hope if he could find all the intermediate Diamonds with the long Clubs. He drew trumps and knocked out the Ace of Diamonds. Then he cashed the remaining Diamond honour and played two more rounds of trumps followed by three Spades. At the end East was squeezed in Diamonds and Clubs.

Note that it does West no good to duck the first round of Diamonds in the hope of destroying the timing for a squeeze, for now declarer can simply throw dummy's last Diamond on a Spade and give up a Club trick as his only loser.

As observed earlier the Lederer Memorial inter-club event is always a fruitful source of good hands. In case readers form the impression that it consists entirely of wild bidding and second-best defence, I will give one well-played hand from the 1973 event. Most pairs reached Six Hearts on the North–South cards—by no means a bad contract, but unmakeable as the cards lie. One declarer, however, with some help from the defence, got home.

The 1973 hand mentioned was as shown on the facing page:

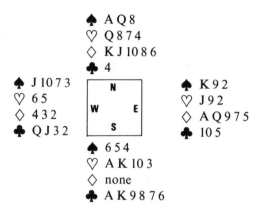

♠ A Q 8
♡ Q 8 7 4
◇ K J 10 8 6
♣ 4

♠ J 10 7 3
♡ 6 5
◇ 4 3 2
♣ Q J 3 2

♠ K 9 2
♡ J 9 2
◇ A Q 9 7 5
♣ 10 5

♠ 6 5 4
♡ A K 10 3
◇ none
♣ A K 9 8 7 6

South dealt at love-all and this was the bidding:

South	West	North	East
1 ♣	pass	1 ◇	pass
1 ♡	pass	2 ♠	pass
4 NT	pass	5 ◇	pass
6 ♡	pass	pass	pass

In the modern style North's Two Spades (where One Spade would have been forcing) agreed Hearts as trumps, showed a Spade control, and suggested a hand too good to raise directly to Four Hearts. The last point is debatable, but it incited South to break the old adage that says: "Blackwood and voids don't mix". He calculated that if his partner held two Aces and a King there would be a good play for Seven Hearts. When partner admitted to one Ace only, however, he settled for the small slam.

West got off to the best lead of a Spade to the Queen and King. There would have been no story if East had played back a Spade, but South's use of Blackwood was still fresh in East's mind. Was it possible, he asked himself, that South had started with six solid Clubs and a singleton Diamond? If so, all dummy's losing Diamonds would go away on the Clubs.

At trick 2 East attempted to cash the Ace of Diamonds. South ruffed with the three of Hearts, played off the Ace of Clubs and ruffed a Club in dummy. He came back to hand with the King of Hearts and led another Club. When West followed with the Jack, declarer had a critical decision to make, but he got it right when he trumped with dummy's Queen of Hearts and followed by finessing the ten of Hearts to land his slam.

It is often said, uncharitably, that some of our finest card players have developed their skill only because their wild bidding lands them in so many near-impossible contracts. Certainly if you reach acrobatic slams you have to play the cards well in an attempt to recover. This was a case in point:

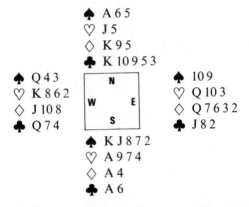

```
                ♠ A 6 5
                ♡ J 5
                ◇ K 9 5
                ♣ K 10 9 5 3
  ♠ Q 4 3       ┌─────────┐       ♠ 10 9
  ♡ K 8 6 2     │    N    │       ♡ Q 10 3
  ◇ J 10 8      │ W     E │       ◇ Q 7 6 3 2
  ♣ Q 7 4       │    S    │       ♣ J 8 2
                └─────────┘
                ♠ K J 8 7 2
                ♡ A 9 7 4
                ◇ A 4
                ♣ A 6
```

In case any children or players of nervous disposition see this book, I shall not give the bidding. It will be sufficient to say that at game-all South ended in Six Spades and West led the Jack of Diamonds.

Declarer won in hand and led a low Heart to the Jack and Queen. He won the Diamond return on the table and followed with three rounds of Clubs, ruffing the third in hand with the seven of Spades to establish the suit. Clearly South wanted to draw trumps, but it was important to end with the lead on the table. It looked impossible, but South saw there was one distribution that might help. If he found West with Q x of Spades, there would be no need to draw the last trump—he could play winning Clubs from dummy until East ruffed in; then South could over-ruff and there would be a trump left on the table to take care of the last Heart. Accordingly South laid down the King of Spades and East followed with the ten. Now there were more problems— if this were a genuine card from Q 10 of Spades the contract was impossible, for West would have 9 4 3 of Spades and the defence would be bound to come to a trump trick.

The only chance, South decided, was that East had started with 10 9 of Spades. (Incidentally, it would be a good false card for East to drop the nine or the ten from an original holding of 10 9 x.) He continued with the Jack of Spades from hand and West (trying desperately to remember whether the two of Spades had already been played) covered with the Queen. Dummy's Ace won and now the last trump was drawn with the six of Spades, declarer triumphantly following suit with the two. Now the winning Clubs could be enjoyed and there were twelve tricks. The key play came very early—when South ruffed the third round of Clubs it was vital for him to keep the two!

The next deal was an intriguing one from rubber bridge. Requiring eight tricks, the early play made it look as though declarer might have to be satisfied with five, but South kept his wits about him and was able to conjure the extra tricks with the aid of what seemed to be double-dummy analysis.

```
                  ♠ A 9 4 3
                  ♡ 7
                  ◇ J 10 8 7 3
                  ♣ 10 8 5
  ♠ K 6                          ♠ J 10 8 7 2
  ♡ Q 10 5 3 2    ┌─────────┐    ♡ J 9
  ◇ 5             │    N    │    ◇ Q 6 4 2
  ♣ Q 6 4 3 2     │ W     E │    ♣ A K
                  │    S    │
                  └─────────┘
                  ♠ Q 5
                  ♡ A K 8 6 4
                  ◇ A K 9
                  ♣ J 9 7
```

South dealt with a 40 part-score and opened One Heart. With the score as an incentive North responded One Spade and South's rebid of Two No-Trumps was passed out. West led the three of Clubs, and the picture when dummy came down was not encouraging. However, East took the King and Ace of Clubs (to which West followed with the two) and the position brightened slightly when it appeared that the defenders could not run their Clubs. At trick 3 East switched to the Jack of Spades and the play went Queen, King and Ace.

With dummy's side entry knocked out there seemed little chance of bringing in the Diamonds unless the Queen fell in two. So South continued with the Ace and King of Diamonds, but West discarded a Club to end declarer's hopes in that direction. Now, however, South had a new idea. If East held only two Hearts, he could be end-played in Spades and Diamonds. With this idea in mind, South cashed the Ace and King of Hearts and led the nine of Diamonds to dummy's ten.

East won with the Queen and did his best by exiting with a Diamond, but when the last Diamond was led he was in difficulties. He was left with 10 8 7 2 of Spades. If he discarded the two, a low Spade from dummy would force him to concede the last trick to the nine. So he discarded the seven, playing his partner for the six. However, declarer led the nine from dummy. East took the ten and cashed the eight, but now dummy's four was good for the eighth trick.

My final example of opportunism arose from that age-old question —deciding whether to play in a major suit fit or in Three No-Trumps. Sometimes, even with a good fit in a major, nine tricks in No Trumps may prove easier, but against that the fact that a side has a good trump suit can often make at least one trick difference in the play, even when there is no obvious way of scoring ruffs.

	♠ Q 10	
	♡ 10 9 8 6	
	♢ A J 8	
	♣ 9 8 7 3	
♠ K J 9 6 4 2		♠ 8 5 3
♡ K 3	N	♡ 7 4 2
♢ 5 4	W E	♢ Q 10 9 3 2
♣ K 10 4	S	♣ Q 6
	♠ A 7	
	♡ A Q J 5	
	♢ K 7 6	
	♣ A J 5 2	

South dealt at love-all and at both tables the bidding started: South, One Heart; West, One Spade; North, Two Hearts; East, pass; South, Three No-Trumps; West, pass.

At one table North, arguing that his Queen of Spades looked a useful card, passed. West led the six of Spades, which gave away a trick, but he got in again with the King of Hearts to clear the Spades and there was no way for declarer to avoid a one-trick defeat.

At the other table North preferred to convert Three No Trumps into Four Hearts and all passed. West made the same opening lead of the six of Spades—not a good choice now; a Diamond would have been better—and dummy's Queen won. A trump finesse lost and West got off play with another Spade to the Ace. South now had the problem of avoiding three losers in the minor suits. To prepare for a possible end-play he cashed the Ace of Clubs. East could see danger ahead—if he followed with a low Club South could draw trumps and put him in with the Queen of Clubs to lead Diamonds—so he unblocked by playing the Queen under the Ace. Now declarer turned his attention to end-playing West. He drew trumps, cashed the King and Ace of Diamonds, and got off play with a Club. West, after cashing two Club tricks, was forced to lead a Spade and conceded a ruff and discard for South's tenth trick.

It is an odd hand when you think about it. North and South have exactly the same distribution, but after the same opening lead the declarer in Hearts was able to gain two tricks in the play over his counterpart playing in No Trumps.

5
Percentages and Odds

Over the years a great deal has been written about percentages at bridge—indeed, whole textbooks have been written on the subject. Some experts delight in wrangling with each other whether a particular line of play in some unlikely slam contract gives a 1 per cent advantage over a simpler and more obvious line. It is a popular misconception that mathematicians automatically make good bridge players. Not so at all; I have known talented mathematicians who are incapable of drawing trumps, and fine bridge players whom you would not trust to tell you the correct time.

It is, however, perfectly true that a basic knowledge of the odds can be of assistance on some hands. Nevertheless, I have always been prepared to forgo the strict odds play if I can see an alternative which might give the opponents more chance to go wrong, for opponents do not always defend perfectly.

Looking back over my files, I can find relatively few deals on which percentages played an important part, although for the scientifically inclined the weekly quizzes sometimes provided grist for their mills. A previous quiz lent its point to the play of the hand that follows—how should a declarer tackle a suit of:

10 9
A K Q 6 2

to give himself the best chance of five tricks. (There are ample entries to both hands.) Clearly the choice lies between finessing the ten on the first round and playing out Ace, King and Queen.

Just consider the possibilities: playing for the drop, as compared with the finesse, gains only when West holds J x x on your left; it loses when West holds x x or x x x x, and obviously these possibilities combined outnumber the other. Note that the chances are not the same as with another familiar combination:

K 4
A Q 10 6 2

Here the finesse of the ten on the second round gains when West holds x x but loses when he holds J x or J x x. On this occasion the play for the drop, other things being equal, is the better chance. The first situation arose on this hand from a semi-final of the Gold Cup:

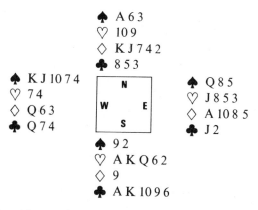

```
                    ♠ A 6 3
                    ♡ 10 9
                    ♢ K J 7 4 2
                    ♣ 8 5 3
  ♠ K J 10 7 4     ┌─────────┐     ♠ Q 8 5
  ♡ 7 4            │    N    │     ♡ J 8 5 3
  ♢ Q 6 3          │ W     E │     ♢ A 10 8 5
  ♣ Q 7 4          │    S    │     ♣ J 2
                   └─────────┘
                    ♠ 9 2
                    ♡ A K Q 6 2
                    ♢ 9
                    ♣ A K 10 9 6
```

North dealt with North–South vulnerable, and the bidding went:

South	West	North	East
		pass	pass
1 ♡	1 ♠	2 ♢	2 ♠
3 ♣	pass	3 ♡	pass
4 ♡	pass	pass	pass

West led the Jack of Spades and after winning with the Ace South had to take an immediate view of the Heart situation. He played off the top Hearts and ended up losing a trick in each suit, to go one down. Jeremy Flint, who played the hand, knows the odds as well as anyone, but there was a further point to consider: if he finesses the ten of Hearts and it loses, Spades will be continued and South will run out of steam. Suppose he ruffs and has to draw three more rounds of Hearts: then he will have no trumps left when he gives up a Club and may easily go three down, vulnerable. It wasn't a happy prospect, but Jeremy's verdict on the hand was that in future he will play to the odds and risk the penalty.

"Two chances must be better than one," was South's obstinate contention after he had been defeated in Six Hearts on the deal below. Of course, it all depends on the nature of the chances. There are certain probabilities of distribution with which all players should be familiar, as they determine the best play on many hands.

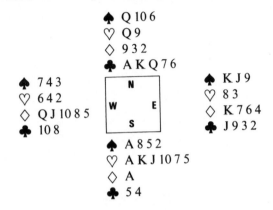

```
                    ♠ Q 10 6
                    ♡ Q 9
                    ◇ 9 3 2
                    ♣ A K Q 7 6
    ♠ 7 4 3           N            ♠ K J 9
    ♡ 6 4 2                        ♡ 8 3
    ◇ Q J 10 8 5    W     E        ◇ K 7 6 4
    ♣ 10 8            S            ♣ J 9 3 2
                    ♠ A 8 5 2
                    ♡ A K J 10 7 5
                    ◇ A
                    ♣ 5 4
```

North was the dealer with North–South vulnerable; bidding was:

South	West	North	East
		1 ♣	pass
2 ♡	pass	3 ♣	pass
3 ♡	pass	4 ♡	pass
6 ♡	pass	pass	pass

Declarer won the Diamond lead, drew trumps, and then played off three top Clubs. When this suit declined to break he had to seek an extra trick from Spades. He played Ace and another, pondered whether to put in the ten or the Queen, and was released from this anxiety when East displayed both King and Jack.

"I took the best chance," said South when his partner showed signs of displeasure. "I wanted either a 3–3 break in Clubs or for just one Spade honour to be right. That must be about ten to one on."

The initial odds were more than six to four against a 3–3 break in Clubs, and it was wrong to say that South wanted just one Spade honour to be right for him. Unless West held a doubleton honour, declarer would have to guess on the second round.

Probably South overlooked the best chance, which was simply to lose a round of Clubs. This will provide a twelfth trick except when the Clubs are 5–1 or 6–0, and the likelihood of that is initially about one in seven. Moreover, as the play progresses, the chance of such an uneven break becomes less.

The next hand produced a lively argument between the declarer and his partner. The issue was simple: should South have played for a 2–2 break in Hearts or for a finesse against the King of Spades?

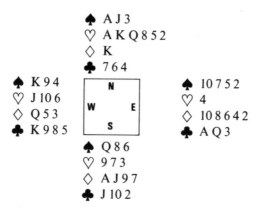

```
               ♠ A J 3
               ♡ A K Q 8 5 2
               ◇ K
               ♣ 7 6 4
♠ K 9 4         ┌─────────┐        ♠ 10 7 5 2
♡ J 10 6        │    N    │        ♡ 4
◇ Q 5 3         │ W     E │        ◇ 10 8 6 4 2
♣ K 9 8 5       │    S    │        ♣ A Q 3
               └─────────┘
               ♠ Q 8 6
               ♡ 9 7 3
               ◇ A J 9 7
               ♣ J 10 2
```

North was the dealer at love-all and the bidding went:

South	West	North	East
		1 ♡	pass
1 NT	pass	3 ♡	pass
3 NT	pass	pass	pass

West led the five of Clubs and the defence began with four rounds of Clubs, dummy discarding a Spade on the fourth round. West then switched to a Diamond. The declarer thought for a while about over-taking the King with the Ace, but finally decided against it. Three top Hearts were played off and West then curtailed proceedings, laying claim to the King of Spades.

"You saw my problem?" South asked. "If the Hearts had been 2–2 I could have got back to hand on the third round and discarded the Spade loser on the Ace of Diamonds."

"The Spade finesse is a 50 per cent chance," replied his partner. "A 2–2 break in Hearts is only a 40 per cent chance. It is true that you have to assume 2–2 or 3–1, but even then it's about 55 per cent in favour of 3–1, better than the finesse."

Listening to these exchanges (I was one of the defenders), it occurred to me that North might have employed a more telling argument. Had East held the King of Spades he would surely have signalled for a Spade lead on the fourth Club. If the King of Spades is wrong and West leads a Spade, the contract can never be made even if the Hearts are 2–2, for declarer can come to hand on the third round of Hearts but cannot get back to dummy. It must be sensible, as West did not exit with a Spade, to assume that the finesse is right.

Even the best of players have an occasional blind spot. The following deal does not seem particularly difficult to play, but neither Robert Jordan, of America, nor Omar Sharif adopted the best line in Six Clubs.

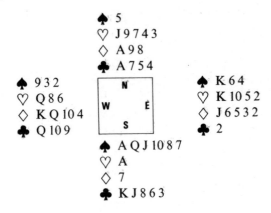

```
                    ♠ 5
                    ♡ J 9 7 4 3
                    ◇ A 9 8
                    ♣ A 7 5 4
     ♠ 9 3 2          ┌─────────┐        ♠ K 6 4
     ♡ Q 8 6          │    N    │        ♡ K 10 5 2
     ◇ K Q 10 4       │ W     E │        ◇ J 6 5 3 2
     ♣ Q 10 9         │    S    │        ♣ 2
                      └─────────┘
                    ♠ A Q J 10 8 7
                    ♡ A
                    ◇ 7
                    ♣ K J 8 6 3
```

These were the two auctions:

South (Jordan)	North (Robinson)
1 ♠	2 ♡
3 ♣	4 ♣
4 NT	5 ♡
6 ♣	pass

South (Sharif)	North (Delmouly)
1 ♠	1 NT
3 ♣	5 ♣
6 ♣	pass

At both tables West began with the King of Diamonds. Declarer won, cashed the Ace of Clubs, and followed with a Club to the King, East discarding a Diamond. Then came the Ace of Spades and a Spade ruff, a Heart to the Ace, and the Queen of Spades.

This was the critical point. Jordan ruffed with dummy's last trump and brought down the King. Sharif let the Queen of Spades run and lost to the King. Both declarers had a guess on the third round of Spades, and all one can say is that Jordan was more happily inspired. The problem lies in how the hand should be tackled at the beginning. The better line is to cash only the Ace of Clubs. Then declarer plays Ace of Spades, Spade ruff, Ace of Hearts, and another Spade. This wins whenever Spades are 3–3, or when the player with four Spades has not more than two Clubs, and also when West has two Spades and three Clubs. It is the old principle: attend to the side suit before drawing all the trumps.

The theme of giving yourself two chances instead of one came up again in the following deal, although it also spotlights how a defender could have restricted declarer's choice of plays and, in all probability, steered him into a losing line of play.

```
                    ♠ 8 5
                    ♡ A K 5 4
                    ◇ A Q J 5
                    ♣ Q J 7
    ♠ A 4 3 2          N           ♠ 10 7 6
    ♡ 7 6 2                        ♡ Q 9 8
    ◇ 9 7 2      W         E       ◇ 8 4 3
    ♣ 9 8 6          S             ♣ 5 4 3 2
                    ♠ K Q J 9
                    ♡ J 10 3
                    ◇ K 10 6
                    ♣ A K 10
```

South played in Six No Trumps and West led the nine of Clubs. Declarer won in dummy and led a Spade to the King and Ace. Now South had two chances for his twelfth trick—he could play for the ten of Spades to fall, and he had the Heart finesse in reserve. What is more, once West had taken his Ace of Spades, there was time to try both possibilities. When the ten of Spades came down on the third round, declarer could table his cards.

It may have been a difficult play for West to find at the table, but if he ducks the King of Spades and follows by ducking the next Spade lead as well South is in difficulties. He *may* find the winning play of leading his last Spade honour to pin the ten of Spades; but he may well prefer to fall back on the straightforward 50 per cent chance of the Heart finesse.

Over the years bridge has established the unenviable reputation of being a quarrelsome game, leading to heated post-mortems, lasting feuds and worse. (Go on, admit it, isn't there a particular player who, above all others, you would like to double for 1700?) The more I think of it, the more I am convinced that it is bridge-players rather than bridge that cause the trouble. I rarely say anything more than "Well done!" or "Bad luck!" to my partners, and the vehemence of a post-rubber discussion that I overheard once startled me. Strolling over, I asked how many declarer had gone down. "Oh, he made his contract," was the reply, "but he missed the best line of play!" This was the hand:

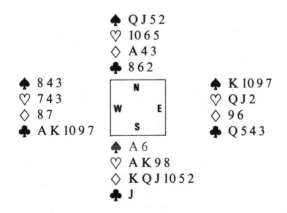

South dealt at game-all and the bidding went as follows:

South	West	North	East
1 ♢	pass	1 ♠	pass
2 ♡	pass	3 ♢	pass
3 ♠	pass	4 ♢	pass
5 ♢	pass	pass	pass

West led the Ace of Clubs and declarer ruffed the Club continuation with the five of Diamonds rather than the two—a good play which costs nothing and may gain as it could lead to a second trump entry to dummy. South drew one round of trumps with the King and followed with three rounds of Hearts. His idea, if the suit did not divide 3–3, was to ruff the fourth round with the Ace of Diamonds.

However, this proved unnecessary and a Spade finesse gave him eleven tricks.

It seemed a very reasonable line of play to me. As the play had gone, North argued, the contract depended on the Spade finesse. It was better to play Ace and another Spade after the first round of trumps. Then if West held the King of Spades there would be two discards for losing Hearts, while if East turned up with the King there was still the chance of a 2–2 trump break when there would be time to play East for both Queen and Jack of Hearts by means of a double finesse.

I give that about a 6 per cent edge over declarer's actual play, technically correct, and as you can see both players succeed, but I never worry too much if my partner makes his contract.

Usually a declarer hopes to find the missing cards in a suit breaking as evenly as possible: indeed, one of the most frequently heard laments in the average card room is, "All we needed was a 3–2 trump break!" It came as quite a surprise when I once heard a quiet voice say "I was lucky to find the trumps 4–0 and a 4–2 diamond break."

The hand appears on the next page:

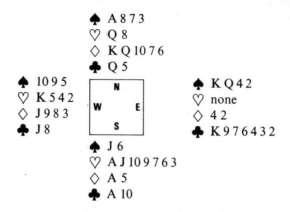

♠ A 8 7 3
♡ Q 8
◇ K Q 10 7 6
♣ Q 5

♠ 10 9 5
♡ K 5 4 2
◇ J 9 8 3
♣ J 8

♠ K Q 4 2
♡ none
◇ 4 2
♣ K 9 7 6 4 3 2

♠ J 6
♡ A J 10 9 7 6 3
◇ A 5
♣ A 10

This was the bidding at game-all, with East–West silent:

South	North
1 ♡	2 ◇
3 ♡	3 ♠
4 ♣	4 ♡
5 ◇	6 ♡
pass	

Against Six Hearts West led the ten of Spades and dummy's Ace won. There seemed two ways of tackling the hand: declarer could go for the 50 per cent chance of the trump finesse or play on Diamonds immediately, hoping for a 3–3 break and a discard. As the second chance was only 36 per cent (and would still leave some work to be done!), South led the Queen of Hearts from the table at trick 2. But East showed out and in an odd way this was to declarer's advantage. Knowing that the trump finesse would lead to immediate defeat, he put up his Ace and started Diamonds by playing Ace and another. When West followed low to the second round South stopped to think. It would not help him now to find Diamonds breaking evenly as there would be no way of escaping a Club loser. The only chance was that West would have to follow to four rounds of Diamonds. As a holding of J x x x was more likely than one of x x x x, declarer finessed dummy's ten of Diamonds on the second round. Now South could take two discards before reverting to trumps.

It is curious to note that a 3–1 trump break, with West holding the King, would have led to almost sure defeat, for South would have had no reason to scorn the percentage play of the trump finesse.

6
Getting the Opposition to Go Wrong

Some players are very knowledgeable about safety-plays, end-plays and other technical manœuvres; others are clever at inducing a mistake from their opponents. It is nice to be good at both but if I had to choose, my money would go on the man who gives the opposition a chance to go wrong. This hand from a team-of-four match proves my point.

```
                    ♠ Q 10 7 4 2
                    ♡ 6 3
                    ◇ A 5
                    ♣ K J 10 4
     ♠ A              ┌─────────┐        ♠ J 9
     ♡ K J 8 4        │    N    │        ♡ 9 7 2
     ◇ Q 10 7 6 4 3   │ W     E │        ◇ K 9 8 2
     ♣ 9 6            │    S    │        ♣ A Q 8 3
                      └─────────┘
                    ♠ K 8 6 5 3
                    ♡ A Q 10 5
                    ◇ J
                    ♣ 7 5 2
```

North dealt with East–West vulnerable and the bidding went:

South	West	North	East
		pass	pass
1 ♠	pass	3 ♣	pass
4 ♠	pass	pass	pass

The bidding may seem a little quaint, but it is in line with modern conventions. The jump to Three Clubs by a player who had passed showed strength in Clubs plus the values for a raise to at least Three Spades; and South (optimistically, perhaps) bid Four Spades, as Three Spades in this sequence would be a sign-off.

The lead at both tables was the six of Diamonds. The first declarer was a player who could turn out double squeezes with the facility of a conjurer producing a rabbit, but his play of this contract was uninspired. He won with the Ace of Diamonds, led a Spade to the King and Ace, and ruffed the next diamond. He led a Spade to the Queen, returned to hand with a trump, and tried the Club finesse. Back came a Heart, the Queen losing the King, and South went one down when the defence made a second Club.

If you examine all four hands you may think there is no way for South to escape defeat. However, the declarer at the second table introduced a slight variation into the play. He also won the Diamond lead with the Ace, but at trick 2 he ruffed a low Diamond instead of leading a low Spade to the King. Then he led the King of Spades—the right shot, for West may hold A J 9. Shorn of his safe Diamond exit, West returned a Heart, which was very understandable if you look at the problem from his angle. So the declarer made his contract. He had been lucky, but he earned it.

Intelligent defence can also play its part, this time in persuading the declarer to go wrong. Looking at the deal below, would you think it made any difference whether East played the King or the Jack of Clubs on a low Club lead against South's contract of Six Spades?

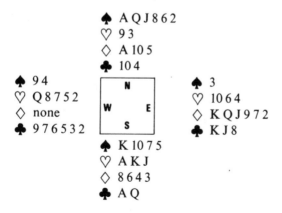

East, the dealer at love-all, was playing weak two-bids, so he began with Two Diamonds and the bidding continued:

South	West	North	East
			2 ◇
dble	pass	3 ◇	pass
3 ♠	pass	5 ♠	pass
6 ♠	pass	pass	pass

North apparently thought that a jump to Four Spades over the double would not represent his values adequately. It was just as well, for the slam cannot be made if East has the lead and West ruffs a Diamond.

As it was, West led a low Club and East's King fell to declarer's Ace. It was obvious that West was void of Diamonds and South reflected that the King of Clubs plus the Diamond suit would be about East's ration for a weak two-bid. He therefore decided to play a loser-on-loser elimination that would depend on West holding the Queen of Hearts. He drew trumps and cashed Queen of Clubs, Ace of Diamonds, and the top Hearts, arriving at this position:

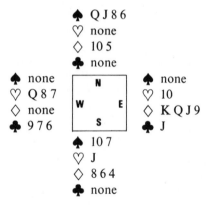

```
                    ♠ Q J 8 6
                    ♡ none
                    ◇ 10 5
                    ♣ none
    ♠ none         ┌─────────┐    ♠ none
    ♡ Q 8 7        │    N    │    ♡ 10
    ◇ none       W │         │ E  ◇ K Q J 9
    ♣ 9 7 6        │    S    │    ♣ J
                   └─────────┘
                    ♠ 10 7
                    ♡ J
                    ◇ 8 6 4
                    ♣ none
```

South led the Jack of Hearts, West played the Queen and a Diamond was discarded from dummy. Now West had to return a Heart or a Club and South was able to dispose of dummy's other Diamond loser.

When a defender who holds K J in a suit can be certain that his partner has not under-led the Ace it is good play to withhold the King. For one thing, the play of the Jack will reveal who holds the Queen. Here the play stands to gain in a different way.

68

When East plays the Jack of Clubs at trick 1, South may place West with the King of Clubs and East with the Queen of Hearts. If he takes that view and finesses the Heart he loses the contract.

Declarer's manoeuvres certainly succeeded in getting the defence to go wrong on the next hand. Or, to be more accurate, succeeded in getting my partner to go wrong, for I was involved at the table and, although it shames my lips to say it, on the losing side. Normally, when your side has had a defensive calamity at the table it is advisable to get your word in first. I am normally no sluggard from the gate, but after this hand, played with one of Britain's lady internationals, I was caught flat-footed. It was rubber bridge.

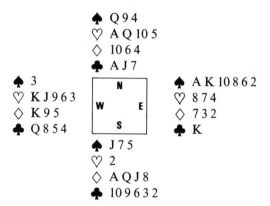

```
                    ♠ Q 9 4
                    ♡ A Q 10 5
                    ◇ 10 6 4
                    ♣ A J 7
    ♠ 3                              ♠ A K 10 8 6 2
    ♡ K J 9 6 3         N            ♡ 8 7 4
    ◇ K 9 5         W       E        ◇ 7 3 2
    ♣ Q 8 5 4          S             ♣ K
                    ♠ J 7 5
                    ♡ 2
                    ◇ A Q J 8
                    ♣ 10 9 6 3 2
```

North was the dealer and neither side was vulnerable. I held the East cards and the bidding went:

South	West	North	East
		1 NT	2 ♠
3 ♣	dble	pass	pass
pass			

No one exactly under-bid. South's Three Clubs was unwise if only because she held good defence against Spades. My partner's double was wholly unjustified, in my opinion; if I have not got the Ace of Spades the defence will collapse.

However, the singleton Spade was led and it will be seen that we can easily take five tricks by way of two Spades, a ruff, a Diamond and at least one high trump. I could tell that the lead was a singleton but it seemed to me premature to give her the ruff at once: it might be important to lead a Diamond through declarer and in any case I expected to come in again with the King of Clubs. So, after winning with the King of Spades, I returned the seven of Diamonds. The declarer studied this for a moment or two, then went up with the Ace and led a trump to the Jack and King. The position was now:

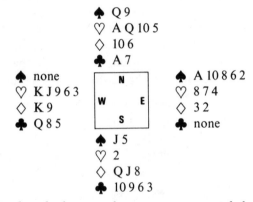

                    ♠ Q 9
                    ♡ A Q 10 5
                    ◇ 10 6
                    ♣ A 7
    ♠ none   ♠ A 10 8 6 2
    ♡ K J 9 6 3   N   ♡ 8 7 4
    ◇ K 9   W   E   ◇ 3 2
    ♣ Q 8 5   S   ♣ none
                    ♠ J 5
                    ♡ 2
                    ◇ Q J 8
                    ♣ 10 9 6 3

Quite pleased with the way things were going, I led the Ace of Spades. My partner went into a small trance. I wasn't worried. I thought she was contemplating a suit-preference signal—a high Heart or a low Heart to tell me whether she wanted the Spade ruff or a Diamond. But her final selection was the King of Diamonds! I gave her the ruff in Spades, but that was the end of the defence as the declarer naturally finessed the ten of Clubs.

While I was still trying to puzzle out what had happened, my partner assailed me for not playing the simple defence of three rounds of Spades. "You must have known I had a singleton!"

The reason for the discard of the King of Diamonds (in case you are still wondering) was that West planned to ruff the third Spade and put me in with the Queen of Diamonds for a ruff in that suit, for two down. She assumed that I held the Queen of Diamonds because declarer had not tried the finesse. . . .

Ah, well—it is a thought; declarer's play of the Ace of Diamonds may have looked odd but it certainly persuaded an experienced defender to go completely astray.

There are moments in life, not only at the bridge table, when the

slightest hesitation can be disastrous. This was one of them—
not that it would not have been difficult for West to set declarer
off on the wrong track if he had played more rapidly:

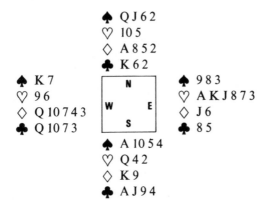

♠ Q J 6 2
♡ 10 5
◇ A 8 5 2
♣ K 6 2

♠ K 7
♡ 9 6
◇ Q 10 7 4 3
♣ Q 10 7 3

♠ 9 8 3
♡ A K J 8 7 3
◇ J 6
♣ 8 5

♠ A 10 5 4
♡ Q 4 2
◇ K 9
♣ A J 9 4

South played in Four Spades after East had made an over-call of
One Heart. West began with the nine of Hearts and the defence
started with three rounds of the suit. When declarer's Queen of
Hearts appeared on the third round West was confronted with an
uncommon, but not unique, problem. If he ruffs with the King
of Spades, dummy will throw a losing Club. If he discards a Diamond, dummy will throw a Club and careful play will win the
contract. The best defence is to ruff with the seven of Spades.
West saw this—but only after a moment's anxiety which revealed
the trump position. South over-ruffed with the Jack of Spades and
led a trump to the Ace, felling the King. The position:

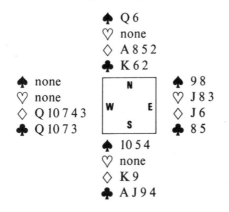

♠ Q 6
♡ none
◇ A 8 5 2
♣ K 6 2

♠ none
♡ none
◇ Q 10 7 4 3
♣ Q 10 7 3

♠ 9 8
♡ J 8 3
◇ J 6
♣ 8 5

♠ 10 5 4
♡ none
◇ K 9
♣ A J 9 4

Declarer still had to avoid the trap of allowing East to make a trump trick by over-ruffing. Knowing that West would be under pressure, he drew two rounds of trumps on which West discarded one Diamond and one Club. Then came King of Diamonds, Ace of Diamonds, and a Diamond ruff, followed by a Club to the King and a fourth Diamond. West won and had to return a club into the A J. The same sort of position would have arisen if West had trumped rapidly at trick 3—except that declarer would have taken a trump finesse, and would have been one trick worse off. . . .

One of the most frequently tried ways of persuading an opponent to go wrong, whether he is declarer or a defender, is to try a false card. Sometimes it works, sometimes it doesn't, but a lot of false cards come under the heading of "play the card that you are known to hold" and, as such, are more or less routine. For example, if a suit is distributed thus:

$$\begin{array}{ccc} & \text{A J x} & \\ \text{Q 10 x} & & \text{x x x} \\ & \text{K 9 8 x} & \end{array}$$

and declarer starts by finessing dummy's Jack, then it is standard practice for West to drop the Queen under the Ace. Declarer may be left with a guess as to the whereabouts of the ten—but if West follows with the ten instead, South has no illusions as to who holds the missing Queen.

Rather less obvious was the manoeuvre tried by East on the following deal:

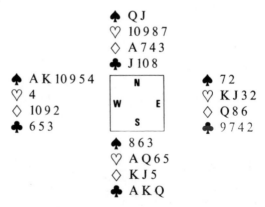

```
                    ♠ Q J
                    ♥ 10 9 8 7
                    ♦ A 7 4 3
                    ♣ J 10 8
  ♠ A K 10 9 5 4          N          ♠ 7 2
  ♥ 4                                ♥ K J 3 2
  ♦ 10 9 2        W         E        ♦ Q 8 6
  ♣ 6 5 3                  S         ♣ 9 7 4 2
                    ♠ 8 6 3
                    ♥ A Q 6 5
                    ♦ K J 5
                    ♣ A K Q
```

At game-all South played in Four Hearts after West had over-called in Spades. West started with three rounds of Spades and dummy ruffed. Thinking quickly, East over-ruffed with the King and switched to Clubs. From South's point of view there was only one entry to dummy and possibly finesses in both red suits. However, it seemed certain that West held the Jack of Hearts so declarer played off the Ace and Queen only to find that he had to lose another trick. If East had made the normal play of over-ruffing with the Jack of Hearts, South would have used the Ace of Diamonds as an entry to finesse in Hearts. Then, after the ten and nine of Hearts had held, he would have had time for the Diamond finesse.

Even more exotic was West's false card on the next hand:

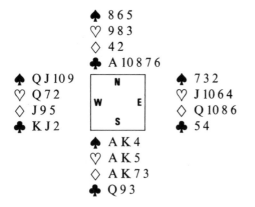

```
              ♠ 8 6 5
              ♡ 9 8 3
              ◇ 4 2
              ♣ A 10 8 7 6
♠ Q J 10 9         N          ♠ 7 3 2
♡ Q 7 2     W          E      ♡ J 10 6 4
◇ J 9 5                       ◇ Q 10 8 6
♣ K J 2           S           ♣ 5 4
              ♠ A K 4
              ♡ A K 5
              ◇ A K 7 3
              ♣ Q 9 3
```

Playing in Three No Trumps on the lead of the Queen of Spades, South had a simple problem—he needed three Club tricks. Winning the opening lead he played the nine of Clubs from hand. He planned to let the nine run and follow by ducking the next round of the suit as well. However, West put up the King of Clubs on the Club lead! It looked for all the world like a singleton King, and if that was the case the only chance was to take the Ace and finesse against East's supposed Jack. But West produced the Jack on the second round and now dummy's Clubs were dead.

Many players regard discarding as a tiresome necessity and believe that if the cards they elect to throw away do not present declarer with his contract it is due to good fortune rather than good management. However, the next two deals, both taken from the 1973 Juan-les-Pins Bridge Festival, are examples of intelligent discarding.

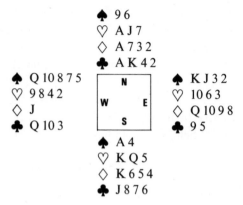

```
                    ♠ 9 6
                    ♡ A J 7
                    ◇ A 7 3 2
                    ♣ A K 4 2
  ♠ Q 10 8 7 5                      ♠ K J 3 2
  ♡ 9 8 4 2          N              ♡ 10 6 3
  ◇ J             W     E           ◇ Q 10 9 8
  ♣ Q 10 3           S              ♣ 9 5
                    ♠ A 4
                    ♡ K Q 5
                    ◇ K 6 5 4
                    ♣ J 8 7 6
```

South dealt at love-all and opened One No Trump. North raised to Three No Trumps, all passed and West led the seven of Spades to the King and Ace. There were eight top winners and declarer decided to play on Clubs. When the Queen did not come down in two rounds the situation did not look hopeful, but South played a third round, thus giving the defenders a chance to go wrong. Declarer hoped that West would win the third Club and, not realizing that Spades were ready to run, might switch. However, East was able to help. The lead of the seven of Spades, assuming that it was fourth highest, placed West with the Queen, ten and eight. The Jack of Spades was not wanted and he threw it on the third Club to solve all his partner's problems.

On the other deal West's discards were designed to confuse declarer rather than aid his partner. In the hand on the next page, North dealt at game-all and South ended in Six Hearts. West led the Queen of Clubs and declarer ruffed the Club continuation. He drew trumps in two rounds and followed with A K of Spades to discard a Diamond. Then came a Spade ruff and West started his deception by dropping the Queen of Spades. Now South played off four more rounds of trumps and it became obvious to everyone, even the waiter, that South had to find the Queen of Diamonds for his contract. With one discard still to go, West was down to the nine of Spades and 7 5 2 of Diamonds. Normally,

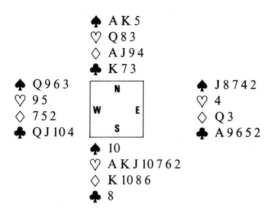

```
              ♠ A K 5
              ♡ Q 8 3
              ◇ A J 9 4
              ♣ K 7 3
♠ Q 9 6 3        N        ♠ J 8 7 4 2
♡ 9 5       W         E   ♡ 4
◇ 7 5 2                   ◇ Q 3
♣ Q J 10 4       S       ♣ A 9 6 5 2
              ♠ 10
              ♡ A K J 10 7 6 2
              ◇ K 10 8 6
              ♣ 8
```

both defenders would avoid any discards in the key suit, but West released the two of Diamonds. South was left with the strong impression that this would have occurred only if West had had no choice. Playing West to have started with four Diamonds, he laid down the King of Diamonds and, when the Queen did not fall, finessed the Jack to lose the last two tricks.

Bridge players are not usually good at conundrums, but the next two hands illustrate the answer to "When is the best defence not the best defence?" The reply, of course, is "When it gets declarer two or more off, but at the same time gives him a chance to make his contract." The first came up in the final of the 1967 Spring Foursomes:

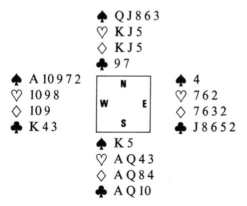

```
              ♠ Q J 8 6 3
              ♡ K J 5
              ◇ K J 5
              ♣ 9 7
♠ A 10 9 7 2     N        ♠ 4
♡ 10 9 8    W         E   ♡ 7 6 2
◇ 10 9                   ◇ 7 6 3 2
♣ K 4 3          S       ♣ J 8 6 5 2
              ♠ K 5
              ♡ A Q 4 3
              ◇ A Q 8 4
              ♣ A Q 10
```

South was the dealer at love-all and the bidding went:

South	West	North	East
2 NT	pass	3 ♠	pass
3 NT	pass	4 NT	pass
6 NT	pass	pass	pass

Against Six No Trumps West led the ten of Hearts to dummy's King, East following with the two to suggest three cards in the suit. Declarer started with a low Spade to the King and Ace, and at this early stage West had a critical play to make. It was clear that his partner held nothing of value and that declarer was marked with practically all the missing high cards. Either he had enough winners for his contract or he would need the Club finesse for his twelfth trick. With the feeling that it didn't matter much, West played a second Heart. Now declarer played off all his red winners before trying the Spades again. On the last, West—in unforeseen trouble—had to bare his King of Clubs in order to keep his guard in Spades. However, South failed to read the position and eventually finessed the Queen of Clubs to lose the last two tricks.

Why was West's defence not the best? Well, if he simply plays back a Spade when he is in with the Ace, declarer can bring no pressure to bear on him. There is no way for South to play off all his red suit winners and still end with the lead on the table, and sooner or later he will be reduced to taking the losing Club finesse. Of course, that would be only one off and rather dull compared with the result that West actually achieved.

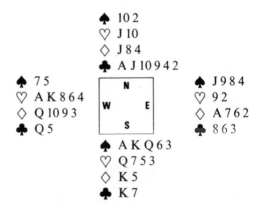

```
              ♠ 10 2
              ♡ J 10
              ◇ J 8 4
              ♣ A J 10 9 4 2
♠ 7 5                          ♠ J 9 8 4
♡ A K 8 6 4      N             ♡ 9 2
◇ Q 10 9 3    W     E          ◇ A 7 6 2
♣ Q 5            S             ♣ 8 6 3
              ♠ A K Q 6 3
              ♡ Q 7 5 3
              ◇ K 5
              ♣ K 7
```

The bidding of the other example with the same theme (opposite page) "had not that repose which stamps the caste of Vere de Vere", but I am only reporting what actually happened at the rubber-bridge table. Furthermore, it was the last rubber of the evening. . . .

South dealt, with North–South vulnerable, and the bidding went:

South	West	North	East
1 ♠	dble	2 ♣	2 ◇
2 ♡	pass	2 ♠	pass
3 ♠	pass	4 ♠	dble
pass	pass	pass	

Against Four Spades doubled West led the King of Hearts. East signalled with the nine and his partner continued with Ace and another Heart. Without much hope, declarer ruffed in dummy with the ten of Spades but East over-ruffed with the Jack. At this point, all East had to do in order to defeat the contract was simply to lay down the Ace of Diamonds, but East was after the big money and switched to the two of Diamonds. As you can see, if declarer has the fortitude to go in with the King he will be in a position to draw trumps and take advantage of the favourable lie of the Clubs to make the remaining tricks. However, the only explanation of events that South could find was that West had most of the outstanding high cards for his bidding, while East had doubled the final contract only because of his length in trumps. Accordingly South played low on the Diamond lead and West won with the Queen. Another Heart lead, ruffed and over-ruffed, was followed by the final indignity of East cashing the Ace of Diamonds and claiming an 800 penalty.

The British team found itself faced with some agonizing decisions at both tables on this deal from their match against China in the 1972 Team Olympiad:

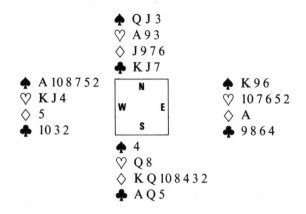

```
                    ♠ Q J 3
                    ♡ A 9 3
                    ◇ J 9 7 6
                    ♣ K J 7
♠ A 10 8 7 5 2      ┌─────────┐      ♠ K 9 6
♡ K J 4             │    N    │      ♡ 10 7 6 5 2
◇ 5                 │ W     E │      ◇ A
♣ 10 3 2            │    S    │      ♣ 9 8 6 4
                    └─────────┘
                    ♠ 4
                    ♡ Q 8
                    ◇ K Q 10 8 4 3 2
                    ♣ A Q 5
```

In the closed room West opened with a weak Two Spades, North passed and East raised defensively to Three Spades. The British South came in with Four Diamonds and was raised to game by North.

Against Five Diamonds West, not unnaturally, led the Ace of Spades and East followed with the nine. At trick 2 West switched to a trump and East won with the Ace. As you can see, the contract is now cold: by playing East for the missing King of Spades declarer can establish a Spade trick to take care of his losing Heart. However, East cunningly returned the six of Spades. He knew that his partner had started with a six-card suit, so the lead could not cost. South took the return at face value: he decided that East had started with only two Spades (perhaps not all that likely on the bidding) and his partner with a seven-card suit. In that case there was only one chance—that West held the King of Hearts. With this hope in mind South ruffed and played off all his minor suit winners in the expectation of squeezing West. But East held the King of Spades and there was no squeeze.

In the open room, the Chinese North became declarer in Three No Trumps and East led the six of Spades. (A Heart lead would have left declarer with no chance.) Now West had a critical play to make. He could play his partner for King to three Spades, in which case the right defence would be to duck the Spade lead completely; or he could hope to take four Heart tricks quickly. West pinned his faith on the Hearts, but his return of the King of Hearts was not a success and declarer came to ten tricks. It is worth noting that if West *does* decide to play Hearts, the best card to lead is the Jack. This will avoid blocking if the suit is distributed so that North holds 9 6 5 4 and East A 10 7 2. The Jack goes to the Ace, the two to the King, and East is left with 10 7 over declarer's 9 6. However, that was a "might-have-been" and Britain lost 730 points on the deal.

Over the years a great deal has been written about deceptive leads. For example, with Q J in trumps, the opening lead of the Jack is an old favourite—declarer, even though he may be missing only four cards may be tempted to finesse on the second round. But have you ever thought of a more advanced possibility—that a lead or play in one suit might persuade declarer to play another suit to your advantage? You may have met this type of situation:

<pre>
                    ♠ 10 5 4
                    ♡ K Q 2
                    ◇ A J 7
                    ♣ K 10 9 5
    ♠ 9 8 6   ┌──N──┐   ♠ A K Q 7
    ♡ 10 7 5 3   │   │   ♡ J 9 6
    ◇ 10 6 4 3   W │   │ E   ◇ 9 8 5
    ♣ 7 4   │ S │   ♣ Q 6 3
                   └─────┘
                    ♠ J 3 2
                    ♡ A 8 4
                    ◇ K Q 2
                    ♣ A J 8 2
</pre>

At game-all South opens One No Trump and North raises to Three No Trumps. West, not fancying his prospects with either red suit, leads the nine of Spades. As East you do best to cash Q, A and K of Spades, then switch to a Heart. Declarer, who needs to find the Queen of Clubs for his contract, will probably finesse into your hand, reasoning that even if you get the lead you can do him no harm, not expecting you to have the last spade.

A neat variation that came up in match play is shown on the next page....

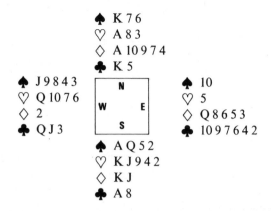

♠ K 7 6
♡ A 8 3
◇ A 10 9 7 4
♣ K 5

♠ J 9 8 4 3
♡ Q 10 7 6
◇ 2
♣ Q J 3

♠ 10
♡ 5
◇ Q 8 6 5 3
♣ 10 9 7 6 4 2

♠ A Q 5 2
♡ K J 9 4 2
◇ K J
♣ A 8

At both tables South became declarer in Six Hearts (perhaps Six No Trumps is slightly safer). One West led the Queen of Clubs and the play was quickly over. South won with the King, cashed the King of Hearts and led a low Heart. When West played low dummy's eight was played, ensuring only one trump loser however the missing cards were distributed.

At the other table West led the two of Diamonds and, although familiar with the safety-play in trumps that had been adopted by his counterpart, South read the lead as a singleton and, to avert the possibility of a ruff, banged out K and A of Hearts. Unlucky. However, it occurred to me that if West had started with, say,

♠ J 9 8
♡ Q 10 7 6
◇ 5 3 2
♣ Q J 3

the lead of the two of Diamonds, looking for all the world like a singleton, might well have dissuaded declarer from taking any safety-play in trumps for fear of a ruff. It is a thought to bear in mind!

To have your opening lead mis-read by partner can be a frustrating experience. Most of us have suffered when we have led the ten from a suit of K 10 9 8 and found J 4 3 2 in dummy. With the best intentions in the world, presumably playing us for a doubleton, our partner encourages the seven from A 7 6 5 and declarer scores with his singleton Queen. Some players have adopted Roman leads (where the lead of an honour tells partner that you have exactly one higher honour in the suit) in an attempt to avoid this sort of disaster, but still things go wrong. Another lead that generally works badly in practice is the under-lead of an Ace against a suit contract, but sometimes it can have surprising results.

The next hand, from rubber bridge, seemed like a fairy tale to West—he under-led an Ace, his partner mis-read the situation, and yet the chapter of accidents led declarer to go completely wrong and fail to make a cast-iron contract.

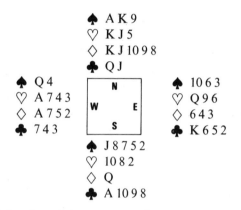

At game-all South ended in Four Spades and West was left with a difficult lead. As the bidding had suggested Heart strength in dummy he chose the three of Hearts and declarer played low from the table. Without much thought East put in the nine and South won with the ten. Trumps were (luckily) drawn in three rounds and declarer continued with the Queen of Diamonds. West won and realizing what had happened at trick 1, led another low Heart.

The play so far had made it apparent to South that West had started with Q x x x in Hearts and East with A 9 x. So he played dummy's Jack; East won with the Queen and returned a Heart to West's Ace. Now a fourth round of Hearts forced South to ruff and, locked in his own hand, he was forced to concede a Club trick in an undignified manner to go one down.

While it is always gratifying to make a contract, it is particularly pleasing to land an impossible one with the aid of a swindle. An

old favourite which comes up from time to time applies to a side
suit in a trump contract. Suppose that Hearts are trumps and the
Spades are distributed like this:

```
                A Q 4 3 2
         10 5              K 8 7 6
                J 9
```

West leads the ten of Spades and South, as declarer, judges that
the King is wrong for him. Rather than take a futile finesse, the
alert player puts up dummy's Ace and drops the Jack from hand.
Then he continues with a low Spade from dummy. East may well
decide that his partner has led from 10 9 5 and fail to go in with
his King.

   Another way of avoiding a finesse that looked sure to be wrong
came up in an Eastbourne Congress some years ago. This was the
hand:

```
                    ♠ Q 6
                    ♡ K Q 6 3
                    ◇ A Q 6
                    ♣ 9 7 6 4
   ♠ 7 5                              ♠ 8 3
   ♡ J 9 5 4        N                 ♡ 10 8 7 2
   ◇ 8 4         W     E              ◇ K 10 9 7 5
   ♣ K 10 8 5 3     S                 ♣ Q J
                    ♠ A K J 10 9 4 2
                    ♡ A
                    ◇ J 3 2
                    ♣ A 2
```

South dealt at game-all and this was the bidding:

South	North
2 ♠	3 ♡
3 ♠	6 ♠
7 ♠	pass

Not very scientific, but after the opening trump lead declarer could
see twelve top tricks and knew that, at worst, his contract would
depend on a Diamond finesse. However, there was no rush to com-
mit himself and South started by playing off four more rounds

of trumps. East signalled heavily in Diamonds and West immediately threw two Diamonds away. Against some opponents you might be suspicious, but on this occasion declarer decided that East–West were transparently honest. What, then, could be done if the Diamond finesse was wrong? South was not a player to give up easily. He cashed the Ace of Clubs and played off his last trump, baring the Ace of Diamonds in dummy. East, with a discard to find from 10 8 7 2 of Hearts and K 10 of Diamonds, decided to part with the ten of Diamonds in order to keep his length in Hearts. Now came a Diamond to the Ace, forcing West to make up his mind whether to discard the King of Clubs or keep his four Hearts. There would have been no story if he had shed a Heart, so you can guess what happened. South triumphantly made the last four tricks with Ace of Hearts, Jack of Diamonds, three of Diamonds and two of Clubs.

The average rubber-bridge player when defending against a slam tends to lose interest. If declarer fails to make his contract, the defender is gratified; if declarer gets home the defender can fall back on blaming the poor cards that he is always dealt. The winning rubber-bridge player, on the other hand, never gives up; even if declarer should be in a position to land his contract, he will always find his task made as difficult as possible. This was a good example of thoughtful defence in an apparently hopeless situation:

```
                    ♠ Q 6 4
                    ♡ A 10 8 7
                    ◇ A K 8
                    ♣ J 5 4
  ♠ 9 8 7 3 2                        ♠ K J 5
  ♡ J 2          ┌──────────┐        ♡ 6 4
  ◇ 10 6 3 2     │ N        │        ◇ Q 5 4
  ♣ 6 2          │ W      E │        ♣ Q 10 9 7 3
                 │    S     │
                 └──────────┘
                    ♠ A 10
                    ♡ K Q 9 5 3
                    ◇ J 9 7
                    ♣ A K 8
```

This was the bidding at love-all:

South	North
	1 NT
3 ♡	4 ◇
6 ♡	pass

North's Four Diamond bid agreed Hearts and showed a maximum No Trump bid. Against Six Hearts West led the nine of Spades to the four, Jack and Ace. Declarer drew trumps in two rounds and then led the ten of Spades to East's King. A lazy player in the East seat would simply push back the ten of Clubs without too much thought, but it is easy to see what would happen. South wins, plays off his remaining trumps (discarding a Club from dummy), and crossing to the King of Diamonds to cash the Ace and the winning Spade. East is forced to unguard one of the minor suits to give declarer his twelfth trick.

Instead, East played back the five of Spades at trick 5. His idea was to force declarer to make his discard on the squeeze card before he was ready. This inconvenienced South, but he was not finished yet. He threw the eight of Clubs from hand and played off winners to come down to Ace of Diamonds and J 5 of Clubs in dummy and J 9 of Diamonds and Ace of Clubs in hand. This was a textbook criss-cross squeeze position—if either opponent had started with both minor suit queens he could not keep them both guarded.

However, East had the last word. He had chosen his discards with great care: four of Diamonds, three, nine and ten of Clubs and five of Diamonds. At the end South had to guess which Queen would fall. Convinced that the Queen of Clubs seemed a more likely candidate, he played off the Ace of Clubs, but East followed with the seven and declarer was a trick short.

Some bridge hands make spectacular kibitzing, although the players at the table may not realize at the time that their decisions are critical. This final example came up in a recent Home Counties' Championship—declarer persuaded the defenders to go wrong in a big way!

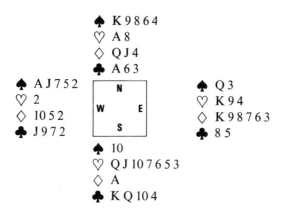

```
                    ♠ K 9 8 6 4
                    ♡ A 8
                    ◇ Q J 4
                    ♣ A 6 3
    ♠ A J 7 5 2        N         ♠ Q 3
    ♡ 2                          ♡ K 9 4
    ◇ 10 5 2      W       E      ◇ K 9 8 7 6 3
    ♣ J 9 7 2        S           ♣ 8 5
                    ♠ 10
                    ♡ Q J 10 7 6 5 3
                    ◇ A
                    ♣ K Q 10 4
```

At one table North opened One Spade, South responded Two
Hearts and North rebid Two Spades. Judging that a slam could
hardly be a good proposition, South settled for Four Hearts and
all passed. The play was rather pedestrian and declarer lost the
two obvious tricks to the Ace of Spades and King of Hearts to
score 450 points.

At the other table the bidding went:

North	South
1 ♠	2 ♣
2 ♠	3 ♡
4 ♡	4 NT
5 ♡	6 ♡
pass	

This requires some explanation: North–South were playing the
Blue Club and South's first two bids were canapé (short suit first)
showing a long Heart suit and possibly no real Club suit. So far,
so good, but South's bid of Four No Trumps was Roman Blackwood and the response of Five Hearts ostensibly showed two aces
of the same colour. Identifying these aces as those of Spades and
Clubs, South pressed on to the small slam.

Now, what about West's opening lead? The Ace of Spades
defeats the contract out of hand but West, not unreasonably,
chose a low Diamond. Dummy played low, East contributed the
six and declarer won with the Ace. Clearly the bidding had gone
wrong—North had made the wrong response to Four No Trumps

—but South was quick to spot his best chance. He led the Queen of Hearts and, when West played low, hopped up with dummy's Ace and led the Queen of Diamonds. Thinking that his play made little difference, East played low and South discarded his losing Spade. Next came the Jack of Hearts and, no matter what East tried, South ran his remaining trumps to squeeze West out of either the Ace of Spades or his Club guard. Very neat, but suppose East covers the Queen of Diamonds with his King? South ruffs and can discard his Spade on the Jack of Diamonds *after reaching dummy with the Ace of Clubs*, but now dummy is entryless and West can simply hold on to his Club guard.

7

Clear Thinking in Defence: 1

It has been said that for every hundred good declarers there is only one good defender. That may be true—there is certainly something to be said for being able to see all of your side's assets at the time you form a plan! Nevertheless, many players would become better defenders if they thought about their problems in the right way.

You will defeat many contracts unexpectedly if you maintain a steady belief that the contract *can* be defeated, somehow. But don't ask for the moon! Think to yourself, what is the *least* that partner can have that will give us a chance? Here are two hands that I noted some years ago during a rubber bridge session:

```
                     ♠ Q 7 2
                     ♡ A K 10
                     ◇ K J 10 8 3
                     ♣ K J
    ♠ K 6                             ♠ 8 5 4
    ♡ J 9 5 4          N             ♡ 8 7 3
    ◇ A 7 6        W       E         ◇ 9 2
    ♣ Q 10 8 2         S             ♣ A 9 6 4 3
                     ♠ A J 10 9 3
                     ♡ Q 6 2
                     ◇ Q 5 4
                     ♣ 7 5
```

This was the bidding:

South	West	North	East
		1 ◇	pass
1 ♠	pass	2 NT	pass
3 ♠	pass	4 ♠	pass
pass	pass		

West led the two of Clubs, the Jack was played from dummy and East won with the Ace. With a resigned air he returned a Club and South made his contract.

If East starts to think in terms of what kind of hand his partner must have to beat the contract, he is bound to come up with the winning play. He must credit West with a high trump and the Ace of Diamonds. On this assumption, a Diamond return at trick 2 establishes four tricks for the defence.

On the second hand the defender asked for too much.

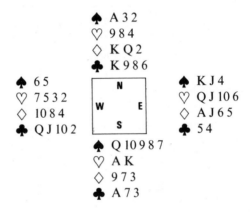

The bidding by South and North was 1 S–2 C; 2 S–4 S. West led the Queen of Clubs to declarer's Ace. South led a Spade to the Ace and returned a Spade. East won with the King and his Queen of Hearts was on the table before he had gathered the previous trick.

The play may seem tempting, but which is the better chance— that West will have a high honour in Hearts or the ten of Diamonds plus a Club trick? Look at it in this light and you will see that the right return is a low Diamond.

On the next deal the East–West players were both experienced performers and they came close to finding a not-so-easy defence. At the critical point East missed a possible inference.

Neither side was vulnerable and North–South had a part-score of 40.

```
              ♠ Q J
              ♡ A Q J 6
              ◇ K 7
              ♣ J 10 7 6 3
♠ K 8 6 4 2        ┌─────────┐        ♠ 10 7 5
♡ 4                │    N    │        ♡ 10 2
◇ A 10 6 5 3       │ W     E │        ◇ J 9 4 2
♣ K 4              │    S    │        ♣ A 9 5 2
                   └─────────┘
              ♠ A 9 3
              ♡ K 9 8 7 5 3
              ◇ Q 8
              ♣ Q 8
```

The bidding went:

South	West	North	East
			pass
1 ♡	1 ♠	2 ♡	2 ♠
pass	pass	3 ♡	pass
pass	3 ♠	4 ♡	pass
pass	pass		

North might have bought the contract more cheaply if he had raised to Three Hearts on the first round.

Distrusting the Spade situation, West opened the Ace of Diamonds and East dropped the two. Suit preference signals on the first round are a debatable affair, but here a signal relating to Diamonds could have little point and West decided that the two suggested a switch to Clubs rather than Spades.

But which Club, the King or the four? If partner held A x x, then a switch to the King of Clubs would lead to a ruff and beat the contract right away. On the other hand, if East held A x x x, a low Club, keeping control of the suit, would be better. A Spade back would set up the King before Clubs were established for declarer.

It struck West in time that if partner held A x x a low Club might still be good enough. Having reached this conclusion he switched to the four of Clubs and East won with the Ace.

Now East went into a trance. Was West hoping for a Club ruff? If West held the Ace of Spades and a singleton Club, only a Club return would beat the contract. So East returned a Club and then the defence could never come to a Spade trick.

Disappointing for West; and East should surely have worked out that if his partner held the Ace of Spades and a singleton Club he would have cashed the Ace of Spades first to make the situation clear. Furthermore, with a singleton Club West might well have preferred that lead to the unsupported Ace of Diamonds.

Most defensive problems can be solved if you ask: what would partner (or declarer!) have done if he had held such-and-such?

"Have you ever seen a worse fate," asked a correspondent, "than befell me on the following hand?"

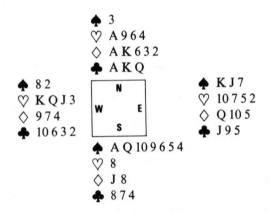

With both sides vulnerable and South the dealer the bidding went:

South	West	North	East
3 ♠	pass	5 NT	pass
7 ♠	pass	pass	pass

Evidently South took his partner's Five No Trumps to be the grand slam force, asking him to bid Seven if he held two of the top three honours in Spades.

North's best bid, probably, would have been Five Spades. As he did not ask about controls the inference would be that his only doubt about a small slam lay in the trump suit. Over Five Spades South would just be worth Six.

However, in Seven Spades West's lead of the King of Hearts was won in dummy and a trump was led, on which East played the seven. South finessed the nine, holding the trick. "You can guess what happened now," said my correspondent, who was East.

Yes, I can. Entering dummy with two Clubs and a Diamond, South ruffed three Hearts. Then came the Ace of Diamonds and a Diamond ruff, leading to this position:

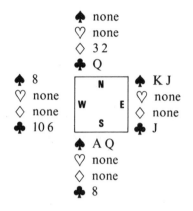

Having lived a charmed life so far, South could expect both opponents to follow to the third Club. When they did, he made the grand slam.

Well played by South, but, as I suggested at the time, didn't it occur to East to false-card with the Jack of Spades on the first round of trumps? That would surely have got him off the hook, for declarer would be bound to try to drop the King of Spades rather than embark on the trump reduction with the ever-present risk of a defender ruffing. Even the King of Spades would probably achieve the same effect. By playing low and letting South win with the nine, East made the position so clear that declarer had to try for his trump reduction.

Here is a chance to compare your defensive play with that of two players in the 1969 World Championship. With East the dealer and East–West vulnerable, these were the hands of North (the dummy) and West:

```
                    ♠ K 4
                    ♡ 10 5 4
                    ◇ Q J 7 6 2
                    ♣ 8 6 4
    ♠ Q 9          ┌─────────────┐
    ♡ K J 9 8 7 6  │      N      │
    ◇ 8 5          │  W       E  │
    ♣ A Q J        │      S      │
                   └─────────────┘
```

The bidding had gone:

South	West	North	East
1 ♣	1 ♡	dble	1 ♠
dble	2 ♡	pass	pass
2 NT	pass	3 NT	pass
pass	pass		

South's opening bid of One Club was conventional, showing a minimum of 17 points, and North's double of One Heart promised a minimum of 6 points. The rest of the bidding was natural. Thus you can place South with a strong, balanced hand, including good Spades.

You lead the eight of Hearts and dummy's ten wins, East playing the two. South leads a Diamond to the Ace and returns the ten, overtaking with the Jack and losing to East's King. Partner leads the seven of Clubs to your Jack. What do you do now? Clearly South has A 10 of Diamonds alone and will not be able to run the suit. His likely distribution is 4–3–2–4. If you decide to exit with the Queen of Spades you will be in the company of the Formosan defender, but you won't defeat the contract, as can be seen by the full hand at the top of the next page.

Forquet, for Italy, won the Spade switch with the Ace and crossed to the King. He played off the Queen of Diamonds, discarding a Spade, then exited in Clubs. West had to lead a Heart either now or later and Forquet made his last Club as well, arriving at nine tricks by way of three Spades, three Hearts, two Diamonds and a Club.

At the other table Belladonna, in the same position, saw that he could afford to give declarer another Heart trick right away. Unless his Spades were as good as A J 10 x (and even then he

```
              ♠ K 4
              ♡ 10 5 4
              ◇ Q J 7 6 2
              ♣ 8 6 4
♠ Q 9          ┌─────────┐        ♠ 10 8 7 6 2
♡ K J 9 8 7 6  │    N    │        ♡ 2
◇ 8 5          │  W   E  │        ◇ K 9 4 3
♣ A Q J        │    S    │        ♣ 10 7 3
               └─────────┘
              ♠ A J 5 3
              ♡ A Q 3
              ◇ A 10
              ♣ K 9 5 2
```

might finesse) South would make only three Spades, three Hearts and two Diamonds. Just a matter of counting tricks—but that is what good defence consists of.

Now try your hand at another World Championship defensive problem that arose when France played America:

```
              ♠ A Q 10
              ♡ K 8 6 5
              ◇ A J 5 3
              ♣ Q 4
♠ K 8 5 3      ┌─────────┐
♡ A 10         │    N    │
◇ Q 8 2        │  W   E  │
♣ K J 6 3      │    S    │
               └─────────┘
```

Stetten, West, opened One Club and North doubled. South responded One No Trump, North raised to Two No Trumps and South bid the game.

West led the Three of Spades, the ten lost to the Jack, and the nine was returned to dummy's Queen. Declarer now led a low Heart from dummy. East played the four and South the nine. How do you plan the defence?

Perhaps it's not too difficult as a problem, but one of the hazards of this game is that one doesn't always know there *is* a problem. In practice, admit it, you would win with the ten of Hearts and exit with a Spade, establishing your King. That is not quite good enough, for this was the full hand:

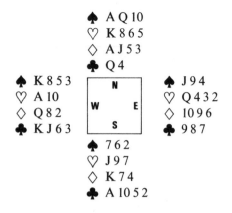

```
                    ♠ A Q 10
                    ♡ K 8 6 5
                    ◇ A J 5 3
                    ♣ Q 4
  ♠ K 8 5 3      ┌─────────┐      ♠ J 9 4
  ♡ A 10         │    N    │      ♡ Q 4 3 2
  ◇ Q 8 2        │ W     E │      ◇ 10 9 6
  ♣ K J 6 3      │    S    │      ♣ 9 8 7
                 └─────────┘
                    ♠ 7 6 2
                    ♡ J 9 7
                    ◇ K 7 4
                    ♣ A 10 5 2
```

If you play the lazy defence, declarer will win the Spade, run four tricks in Diamonds, and exit with a Heart to the Ace. You make your King of Spades but then have to open up the Clubs. South makes the last three tricks with two Clubs and the King of Hearts. Foreseeing this, Stetten won with the ten of Hearts and cashed the Ace before exiting with a Spade. Then he could sit back and wait for two more tricks.

It is a terrible thing to make a carefully considered play that covers every possibility but one, and then find that you could have covered this extra possibility as well. Consider this defensive situation:

```
                    ♠ J 7 4
                    ♡ 10 6 2
                    ◇ Q J 9 6 5 2
                    ♣ Q
                 ┌─────────┐      ♠ K 10 8
   ♡ 9 led       │    N    │      ♡ K Q J 7 5
                 │ W     E │      ◇ K 10 4 3
                 │    S    │      ♣ 9
                 └─────────┘
```

At game-all the bidding has gone:

South	West	North	East
		pass	1 ♡
2 ♠	3 ♣	3 ♠	pass
4 ♠	pass	pass	pass

West leads a Heart to the declarer's Ace. A low Club is taken by West's Ace, and two more rounds of Hearts are played, South ruffing the third round. A low Club is ruffed, by the seven and over-ruffed by the eight. East now sees:

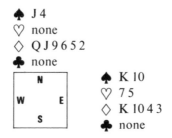

♠ J 4
♡ none
◇ Q J 9 6 5 2
♣ none

♠ K 10
♡ 7 5
◇ K 10 4 3
♣ none

What should he play now? East, a good player, worked it out like this: "South must have at least six Spades to the Ace Queen, he has shown two Hearts, and probably has four Clubs, plus the singleton Ace of Diamonds. I mustn't let him get to dummy to take the Spade finesse. If I play a Diamond he must come to my King of Spades." So East exited with a low Diamond, but, alas, partner had *eight* Clubs and the full hand was:

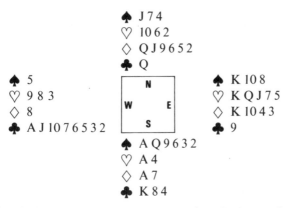

♠ J 7 4
♡ 10 6 2
◇ Q J 9 6 5 2
♣ Q

♠ 5
♡ 9 8 3
◇ 8
♣ A J 10 7 6 5 3 2

♠ K 10 8
♡ K Q J 7 5
◇ K 10 4 3
♣ 9

♠ A Q 9 6 3 2
♡ A 4
◇ A 7
♣ K 8 4

South let the Diamond run to dummy and took the Spade finesse to make his contract. Obviously the *King* of Diamonds from East would have done the trick. South cannot enter dummy because the next Diamond will be ruffed by West.

Say you hold the East hand below at game-all and South opens with Four Spades, which West and North pass. It is certainly not

clear what you should bid at this point, for anything you elect
to do may turn out well or badly, depending on how your partner
is fixed.

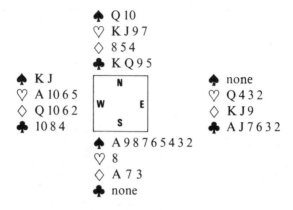

```
              ♠ Q 10
              ♡ K J 9 7
              ◇ 8 5 4
              ♣ K Q 9 5
♠ K J         ┌─────────┐        ♠ none
♡ A 10 6 5    │    N    │        ♡ Q 4 3 2
◇ Q 10 6 2    │ W     E │        ◇ K J 9
♣ 10 8 4      │    S    │        ♣ A J 7 6 3 2
              └─────────┘
              ♠ A 9 8 7 6 5 4 3 2
              ♡ 8
              ◇ A 7 3
              ♣ none
```

As it happens, your best move is to pass Four Spades, so let's
assume you are clever enough to follow that course of action.
West leads the two of Diamonds and South wins your King with
the Ace. Declarer plays the Ace of trumps, your partner producing the Jack, and now you have your second problem: what should
you discard on the Ace of Spades. You may think that you could
readily spare a medium Club. It is true that, in itself, a Club is as
dispensable as yesterday's newspaper, but it won't tell your
partner what he really needs to know.

Actually, there is only one correct discard—the Queen of
Hearts! If you make this play the contract is sure to go down,
for whenever declarer leads a Heart your partner will grab the Ace
and lead Diamonds to put the contract one down. If you were to
play any other card on the Ace of Spades, and declarer were to
lead a Heart at trick 3, it is by no means certain that your partner
would rise with the Ace. He might reasonably decide to duck on
the basis that declarer, with a doubleton Heart, might mis-guess.

The point is that you know more about the hand than your
partner. You learn from the play of the Jack of Spades at trick 2
that declarer started with nine Spades, and you assume from
West's lead of the two of Diamonds that declarer has two Diamonds to lose. It follows from this that South cannot possibly

have more than one Heart, and you must therefore play the Big Brother role to stop partner from making a mistake.

When your partner leads the Ace of a suit against No Trumps, which card do you play from x x x? On the general principle that a high card is more encouraging than a low one, I have always played the top card from three when it looks as though partner may have led from A K J x x and wants to know, perhaps, whether the declarer holds Q x or Q x x. However, I find that some players expect you to play high-low with a doubleton. I suppose there is something in it; if the understanding is that you high-low from an even number, partner will usually be able to tell whether you hold two, three or four. These reflections arose from the following hand:

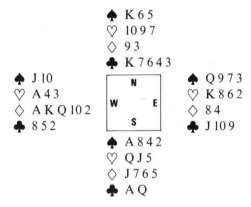

```
              ♠ K 6 5
              ♡ 10 9 7
              ◇ 9 3
              ♣ K 7 6 4 3
♠ J 10            N           ♠ Q 9 7 3
♡ A 4 3                       ♡ K 8 6 2
◇ A K Q 10 2  W       E       ◇ 8 4
♣ 8 5 2           S           ♣ J 10 9
              ♠ A 8 4 2
              ♡ Q J 5
              ◇ J 7 6 5
              ♣ A Q
```

South dealt at game-all and, playing a weak No Trump throughout, opened One No Trump. Pressing a little, West doubled and all passed. West led the Ace of Diamonds and East played the eight. Reading this for a doubleton, West switched to the Jack of Spades. Declarer then ran seven tricks by way of two Spades and five Clubs.

It was an instructive position for the defence. The Spade switch may look attractive, but the way to look at it is this: "The declarer may be able to run five tricks in Clubs. If he has the Ace of Spades as well, and I switch to a Spade, he will make his contract. Meanwhile, partner may hold the King of Hearts, in which case we can make two Hearts and five Diamonds. A low Heart will not in any event be fatal, for if South has the King of Hearts he won't be able to make more than six tricks in Clubs and Hearts; so we will still be safe if partner has the Ace of Spades and another Diamond." In short, a Heart switch beats the contract if partner holds either King of Hearts or Ace of Spades.

The next deal came from the 1971 American trials and led to a great deal of heart-burning. See if you sympathize with the defender. . . .

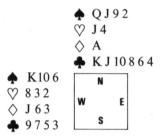

```
              ♠ Q J 9 2
              ♡ J 4
              ◇ A
              ♣ K J 10 8 6 4
  ♠ K 10 6    ┌─────────┐
  ♡ 8 3 2     │    N    │
  ◇ J 6 3     │ W     E │
  ♣ 9 7 5 3   │    S    │
              └─────────┘
```

West was the dealer and, with North–South vulnerable, the bidding went:

South	West	North	East
	pass	1 ♣	1 ◇
1 ♡	pass	1 ♠	pass
3 ♡	pass	4 ♡	pass
pass	pass		

West led a low Diamond, won by dummy's Ace. Declarer came to hand with the Ace of Hearts, led the Queen of Diamonds and ruffed it, then played a low Club from the table. East played the Ace and South the Queen. East then switched to the Ace and eight of Spades, declarer playing the three and four. West is in with the King of Spades. What is he to do? Does partner want a Spade ruff, or can you hope to find him with a singleton Club? Remembering that North had bid Spades and had not been supported, West returned a Club. Alas for him, the whole deal was:

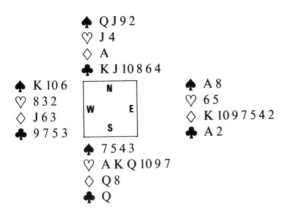

```
                    ♠ Q J 9 2
                    ♡ J 4
                    ◇ A
                    ♣ K J 10 8 6 4
♠ K 10 6        ┌─────────┐    ♠ A 8
♡ 8 3 2         │    N    │    ♡ 6 5
◇ J 6 3         │ W     E │    ◇ K 10 9 7 5 4 2
♣ 9 7 5 3       │    S    │    ♣ A 2
                └─────────┘
                    ♠ 7 5 4 3
                    ♡ A K Q 10 9 7
                    ◇ Q 8
                    ♣ Q
```

"I couldn't tell whether you were short in Spades or Clubs," pleaded West. But in a high-class game you don't escape with that sort of argument. "If I had wanted a Club ruff," East pointed out, "I wouldn't have put you on the spot by leading Ace and another Spade: I would have led a low Spade immediately so that a Club would be the only possibility."

In the area of defence, technique will take you only half-way: imagination and alertness are needed as well. Here is an example where all three qualities come into play:

```
                    ♠ Q 4
                    ♡ Q 9 6 2
                    ◇ K Q 10 7 6 2
                    ♣ 3
♠ A J 2         ┌─────────┐    ♠ 10 6 5
♡ K 10 4        │    N    │    ♡ A J 7 5
◇ 5             │ W     E │    ◇ J 8 4
♣ Q J 10 9 7 2  │    S    │    ♣ 6 5 4
                └─────────┘
                    ♠ K 9 8 7 3
                    ♡ 8 3
                    ◇ A 9 3
                    ♣ A K 8
```

With South the dealer and North–South vulnerable the bidding goes:

South	West	North	East
1 ♠	2 ♣	2 ◇	pass
2 NT	pass	3 NT	pass
pass	pass		

South's rebid of Two No Trumps is not exactly classical, with two small Hearts, but as he has the top Clubs and the Ace of Diamonds it is reasonable to conclude that partner will have some values in Hearts.

West leads the Queen of Clubs and declarer notes that he has eight tricks (barring four Diamonds on his right, which may lead to entry trouble). It looks as though the best plan is to set up a ninth trick in Spades while there are still entries to both hands, so South wins with the Ace of Clubs and leads a low Spade.

Most players in the West position would inertly contribute the two at this point and then see declarer run swiftly for home with six Diamonds and three side winners.

On most occasions it wouldn't be good play at all to beat the air with the Ace of Spades, but here a little reflection will show that West must not allow the Queen to win. South surely has the Ace and King of Clubs and his failure to play on Diamonds is most significant: South must hold the Ace, for otherwise he would be developing this suit first.

The setting tricks can be found only in Hearts and here technique will come to West's aid. After nipping in with the Ace of Spades he must lead the ten of Hearts. Dummy's Queen is covered by the Ace, and let us hope that East will not let the side down at this point. He must return a Heart to the King, and then the four of Hearts, through dummy's 9 6, gives the defence two more tricks.

8
Clear Thinking in Defence: 2

Here is a testing problem in defence. Suppose you are East on the deal below, defending against Five Diamonds after South has bid Hearts and Diamonds. Partner leads a Club and you cash the King and Ace. What do you play next?

```
                    ♠ A Q 10 7 5 2
                    ♡ 7 5
                    ◇ 8 6 3
                    ♣ 9 6
    ♠ J 9 6                             ♠ K 8 3
    ♡ 9 8 4 2        ┌──────────┐       ♡ J 6
    ◇ 10             │    N     │       ◇ J 7 5 4
    ♣ Q 10 8 4 3     │ W     E  │       ♣ A K 7 2
                     │    S     │
                     └──────────┘
                    ♠ 4
                    ♡ A K Q 10 3
                    ◇ A K Q 9 2
                    ♣ J 5
```

With both sides vulnerable the bidding had gone:

South	West	North	East
1 ♡	pass	1 ♠	pass
3 ◇	pass	3 ♠	pass
4 ◇	pass	5 ◇	pass
pass	pass		

North's bid of Five Diamonds was not well-judged—he should have aimed at ten tricks in Hearts rather than eleven in Diamonds.

After cashing two Club tricks East exited with a low Heart. The declarer went up with the Ace and played off the Ace and King of Diamonds, West showing out on the second round. It was then an easy matter for South to enter dummy with a Spade and pick up the Jack of Diamonds. As no doubt you will have realized by

101

now, East's lead of a Heart at trick 3 was a lazy man's play. The best return was a low Spade. This removes the only entry to dummy before South has discovered the Diamond position and ensures a trick for East's Jack of Diamonds.

For the most part you don't have to be clever at bridge to be a good winner. If you simply avoid obvious errors you will be better than most. But there are times—and the hand below is one of them—when you have to step out of line and do something dynamic.

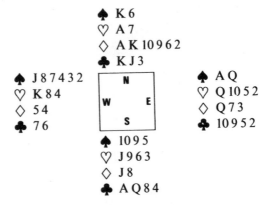

```
                    ♠ K 6
                    ♡ A 7
                    ◇ A K 10 9 6 2
                    ♣ K J 3
  ♠ J 8 7 4 3 2        N          ♠ A Q
  ♡ K 8 4                         ♡ Q 10 5 2
  ◇ 5 4        W           E      ◇ Q 7 3
  ♣ 7 6                S          ♣ 10 9 5 2
                    ♠ 10 9 5
                    ♡ J 9 6 3
                    ◇ J 8
                    ♣ A Q 8 4
```

North was the dealer at love-all. There is much to be said for opening Two No Trumps on the North hand, but he chose the more orthodox One Diamond. South responded One No Trump and North raised to Three No Trumps.

The Spade lead from West, which spelt doom to dummy's King, illustrates my point about opening Two No Trumps instead of One Diamond. However, the Spades were blocked on this occasion. After making the Ace and Queen of Spades East switched to a low Heart and the nine was covered by the King and Ace. When East came in with the Queen of Diamonds he cashed his Queen of Hearts but that was the end of the defence.

Do you see where the defence failed? East needs to find his partner with either the King of Hearts or the Ace of Clubs, and clearly he should try the Hearts first. But to be sure of establishing the King of Hearts as an entry, he must lead the Queen, not a low one. That forces out the Ace, on this round or the next, and West comes in later to make his good Spades. The play of the Queen of Hearts is a *Deschapelles Coup*, named after a Frenchman who was a master at both chess and whist.

The play in the trump suit was critical at both tables when the following hand was played in the 1972 Olympiad.

```
                    ♠ A 10 9
                    ♡ 10 9 3
                    ◊ A K J 10 8
                    ♣ 10 4
   ♠ K J 6 3      ┌──────────┐      ♠ 7
   ♡ K 7 4        │    N     │      ♡ A J 8 6 2
   ◊ Q 4          │ W      E │      ◊ 3
   ♣ K 6 3 2      │    S     │      ♣ A Q J 9 8 7
                  └──────────┘
                    ♠ Q 8 5 4 2
                    ♡ Q 5
                    ◊ 9 7 6 5 2
                    ♣ 5
```

South dealt with East–West vulnerable when the deal came up in the match between the ladies of Sweden and USA. This was the bidding, with America North–South:

South	West	North	East
pass	pass	1 ◊	2 NT
3 ◊	3 ♠	pass	4 ♣
pass	4 ♡	pass	pass
pass			

East's Two No Trumps was a variant of the Unusual No Trump— showing, over a minor suit opening, the other minor and Hearts. West's Three Spades is hard to explain but had a lucky influence on the final contract. Both North and South felt that their opponents had had a misunderstanding so neither was tempted to save in Five Diamonds. Against Four Hearts North started with two top Diamonds and declarer ruffed in dummy. A Heart to the King was followed by a low Heart and when North played small the play of the Jack of Hearts from dummy would have ensured one trump loser at most, and the contract. But declarer, concerned with the possibility of a Club ruff, put up the Ace of Hearts to drop the Queen. This led to eleven tricks.

At the other table South was more imaginative:

South	West	North	East
pass	pass	1 $\diamondsuit$	2 NT
3 ♠	4 $\heartsuit$	4 ♠	pass
pass	dble	pass	pass
pass			

Against Four Spades doubled West led a low Heart to the Ace. East switched to Ace and another Club, declarer ruffed and led a low Spade from hand. Correctly, West put in the Jack. Declarer took the Ace and continued with the ten of Spades. Incorrectly, West held off hoping to keep control in the trump suit. Now South abandoned the trumps to play on Diamonds and West could come to only two trump tricks and the King of Hearts. That was two off and a good save against a vulnerable game, but West could have done better. If she wins the second round of trumps and forces declarer with King and another Heart there is no way for South to avoid the loss of two more trump tricks. If she plays on Diamonds West ruffs and gives a ruff and discard: then South cannot draw the last trump and West scores yet another trick.

A lot has been written over the years on the topic of leading trumps. Players often used to lead trumps when they simply could not think of anything better to do, but nowadays they tend to be better disciplined about the whole affair. Perhaps it is just a personal opinion, but at least my rubber-bridge partners have refrained from leading their singleton trumps and so enabling declarer to pick up J 10 x x or Q 10 x x from my hand without loss.

On the next deal West led a trump for a sensible, constructive reason. He suspected, rightly, that without a trump attack declarer would be able to score a ruff on the table. However, a moment's inattention later on gave back everything that he had gained. These were the hands:

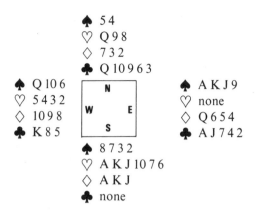

```
              ♠ 5 4
              ♡ Q 9 8
              ◇ 7 3 2
              ♣ Q 10 9 6 3
  ♠ Q 10 6       ┌─────────┐       ♠ A K J 9
  ♡ 5 4 3 2      │    N    │       ♡ none
  ◇ 10 9 8     W │         │ E     ◇ Q 6 5 4
  ♣ K 8 5        │    S    │       ♣ A J 7 4 2
                 └─────────┘
              ♠ 8 7 3 2
              ♡ A K J 10 7 6
              ◇ A K J
              ♣ none
```

South dealt, with East–West vulnerable, and this was the bidding:

South	West	North	East
1 ♡	pass	2 ♡	dble
4 ♡	pass	pass	pass

You may not think highly of North's raise to Two Hearts—a pass would certainly have escaped criticism—but it led to a fair contract of Four Hearts. West could judge from the bidding that a trump lead could hardly damage any holding in his partner's hand and might serve to reduce dummy's ruffing power, so he led the five of Hearts. He was very much on the right track: on any other lead it is easy to see that declarer can come to one Spade ruff in dummy and follow with the Diamond finesse to give himself ten tricks.

After the trump lead things did not look too bright for South. Even assuming that the Diamond finesse was right it looked as though the defenders would be one tempo ahead if South still tried to ruff a Spade. Nevertheless, South still tried the two of Spades from hand at trick 2. Caught off balance, West followed with the six and was horrified to see his partner overtake. With no trumps, East was powerless to prevent an eventual Spade ruff.

It should not have been difficult for West to foresee this happening. It is hard to construct a hand where the play of the ten of Spades at trick 2 could cost, but all too easy to see how the play of a low Spade could lead to disaster.

The next two hands have a common theme—an opportune switch by a defender to remove one of declarer's entries before he is ready to use it. However, both plays were difficult and missed at the table. This was the first:

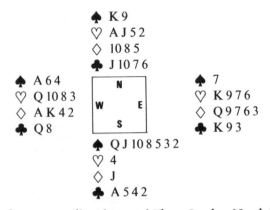

```
              ♠ K 9
              ♡ A J 5 2
              ◇ 10 8 5
              ♣ J 10 7 6
♠ A 6 4                        ♠ 7
♡ Q 10 8 3         N           ♡ K 9 7 6
◇ A K 4 2     W         E      ◇ Q 9 7 6 3
♣ Q 8              S           ♣ K 9 3
              ♠ Q J 10 8 5 3 2
              ♡ 4
              ◇ J
              ♣ A 5 4 2
```

South dealt at game-all and opened Three Spades. North hopefully raised to game and all passed. Against Four Spades West led the King of Diamonds and declarer ruffed the Diamond continuation. A Spade to the King was allowed to win but West won the next trump lead and played a third Diamond. South ruffed, drew the last trump and led a low Club from hand. West took his Queen (it does not help to play low), but South was able to cross to the Ace of Hearts and finesse in Clubs to come to ten tricks.

Do you see what West missed? He must play a Heart when in with the Ace of Spades: then dummy's entry is removed before South can use it profitably and the Clubs cannot be brought in.

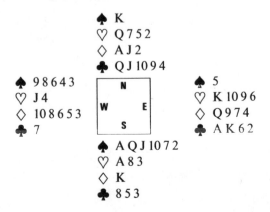

```
              ♠ K
              ♡ Q 7 5 2
              ◇ A J 2
              ♣ Q J 10 9 4
♠ 9 8 6 4 3                    ♠ 5
♡ J 4              N           ♡ K 10 9 6
◇ 10 8 6 5 3  W         E      ◇ Q 9 7 4
♣ 7                S           ♣ A K 6 2
              ♠ A Q J 10 7 2
              ♡ A 8 3
              ◇ K
              ♣ 8 5 3
```

In the companion deal, shown at the foot of the opposite page, East opened One Club and after some unconvincing bidding South ended in Four Spades which West doubled. West led his singleton Club, and the King followed by the Ace exposed the position. As he was better placed for a Heart return rather than a Diamond, East played back the six of Clubs (suggesting an interest in the higher-ranking suit) for West to ruff. The Jack of Hearts went to the Queen, King and Ace, but now South was able to draw trumps in four rounds. Then he over-took the King of Diamonds with dummy's Ace and threw his losing Hearts on the two good Clubs.

This time it was East who was not thinking clearly enough. If West holds a high Heart or a trump trick it doesn't matter which Club he returns, but if not, the only chance is to find declarer with a singleton Diamond. After a return of the two of Clubs for West to ruff and a *Diamond* back, East can sit and wait for his Heart tricks. There is no point in South over-taking with the Ace of Diamonds while West still has his trumps left.

You might think that there would be a uniformly high standard of defence in an event like the *Sunday Times* Bridge Championship, but I'm afraid that that is not always the case. During the 1974 event the following intriguing deal arose, and despite the high-class field, a moment's careless thought by several Easts spelt disaster.

```
                      ♠ 4 3 2
                      ♥ 10 8 6
                      ◇ K 6
                      ♣ A 10 7 4 2
      ♠ K 8 6 5                        ♠ J 10 9
      ♥ 3             ┌─────────┐      ♥ 4 2
      ◇ 10 9 8 7 4    │ N       │      ◇ A Q 3 2
      ♣ J 8 6         │ W     E │      ♣ K Q 9 3
                      │    S    │
                      └─────────┘
                      ♠ A Q 7
                      ♥ A K Q J 9 7 5
                      ◇ J 5
                      ♣ 5
```

Try it yourself, with the advantage of seeing all four hands. South ends in Four Hearts and your partner leads the ten of Diamonds.

It is easy enough to take two Diamond tricks, but what is the correct switch at trick 3? The natural inclination is to push through the Jack of Spades, up to the weakness on the table, but now an alert declarer can get home. South should reason that as there is no hurry to try the Queen of Spades (he can always lead low towards the Queen later) he can afford to win with the Ace and try the Clubs. The play continues with a Club to the Ace and a Club ruffed high in hand. Dummy is entered twice more with the six and eight of Hearts for two more Club ruffs. Then the thirteenth Club is established for South's tenth trick.

Did you see the killing defence? East should play back a trump at trick 3 rather than the Jack of Spades. This takes away a vital trump entry to the table before South is ready to use it. Eventually declarer, who can no longer bring in the Clubs, has to fall back on a losing Spade finesse.

A defender holding four trumps can play a forcing game with a long side suit, even if he concedes a ruff and discard. If West is defending against Four Spades here,

```
                     ♠ J974
                     ♡ J5
                     ◇ AQ9
                     ♣ KJ43
   ♠ A532          ┌─────────┐        ♠ 6
   ♡ AK874        │    N    │       ♡ 10962
   ◇ 85           │ W     E │       ◇ 7432
   ♣ 107          │    S    │       ♣ 9852
                   └─────────┘
                     ♠ KQ108
                     ♡ Q3
                     ◇ KJ106
                     ♣ AQ6
```

he simply plays three rounds of Hearts. It does not matter where declarer ruffs: West wins the third round of trumps and forces with another Heart to defeat the contract.

(After I put this analysis in the weekly column, several readers pointed out that it is not quite correct: a Diamond discard from dummy can still lead to ten tricks with careful timing. Thank you, but the principle is still a good one.)

Somehow the same sort of situation is not so easy to diagnose when a defender holds a singleton trump. Take this hand from the 1969 European Championships in Oslo:

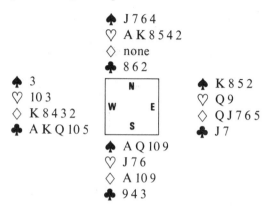

♠ J 7 6 4
♡ A K 8 5 4 2
♢ none
♣ 8 6 2

♠ 3
♡ 10 3
♢ K 8 4 3 2
♣ A K Q 10 5

♠ K 8 5 2
♡ Q 9
♢ Q J 7 6 5
♣ J 7

♠ A Q 10 9
♡ J 7 6
♢ A 10 9
♣ 9 4 3

West dealt at game-all and this was the bidding:

South	West	North	East
	1 ♢	dble	2 NT
3 ♠	4 ♣	4 ♠	dble
pass	pass	pass	

You may not be charmed with North's first-round double—I'm not, but there it is.

West started with three top Clubs and on the third East discarded the nine of Hearts. West switched to a Heart and declarer was home, but note the effect of playing a fourth Club. Say declarer ruffs in dummy—East discards the Queen of Hearts and now, whatever South tries, he cannot pick up East's trumps.

The problem of which card to lead from a broken suit when you are attempting to set up a ruff for your partner is always interesting. For example, how should East–West defend against a Spade contract by South on the deal shown at the top of the following page?

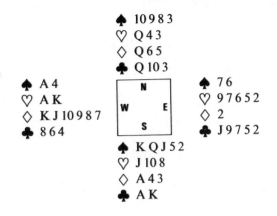

```
              ♠ 10 9 8 3
              ♡ Q 4 3
              ◇ Q 6 5
              ♣ Q 10 3
♠ A 4                        ♠ 7 6
♡ A K         N              ♡ 9 7 6 5 2
◇ K J 10 9 8 7  W   E        ◇ 2
♣ 8 6 4         S            ♣ J 9 7 5 2
              ♠ K Q J 5 2
              ♡ J 10 8
              ◇ A 4 3
              ♣ A K
```

To make the maximum West cashes two top Hearts, then switches to the King of Diamonds. South wins and starts on trumps but West takes the Ace of Spades and leads the Jack of Diamonds for his partner to ruff dummy's Queen. Then West takes his Heart ruff and can cash the ten of Diamonds. Note that it is not good enough to lead the Jack of Diamonds at trick 3—dummy's Queen wins the trick and when East later ruffs a Diamond it is only a loser that he is trumping.

The next hand from match play makes an interesting "dual".

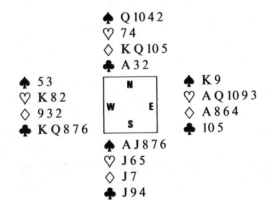

```
              ♠ Q 10 4 2
              ♡ 7 4
              ◇ K Q 10 5
              ♣ A 3 2
♠ 5 3                        ♠ K 9
♡ K 8 2       N              ♡ A Q 10 9 3
◇ 9 3 2       W   E          ◇ A 8 6 4
♣ K Q 8 7 6     S            ♣ 10 5
              ♠ A J 8 7 6
              ♡ J 6 5
              ◇ J 7
              ♣ J 9 4
```

East opened One Heart. West raised to Two Hearts and after two passes South protected, rather daringly, with Two Spades. Eventually he played in Three Spades and West led the two of Hearts. East won with the Queen (good technique) and pushed through the ten of Clubs to the Jack and Queen. Now it was declarer's turn to make a good play—he allowed the Queen of Clubs to hold.

How should West continue? If he plays another Heart he will never get in to make a second Club trick, while a Diamond or a trump gives declarer plenty of time to establish a Diamond in dummy for a Club discard. Nor will the King of Clubs hold now—South can simply draw trumps. The solution is neat—West must give up thoughts of a second Club trick and return a *low* Club. If declarer wins with dummy's Ace there are five losers (and the defenders can get at their tricks!), and if he wins in hand he cannot get to dummy. Eventually West gets in with the King of Hearts and gives his partner a Club ruff for the setting trick.

The play of the Jack by a defender from a holding of Jack and another is one that can sometimes have a surprising effect on declarer's communications. Consider this example:

```
              ♠ 6 4 3
              ♡ 4 3
              ◇ A 9 8 7 3
              ♣ 6 4 2
  ♠ 9 2           N           ♠ Q J 10 8 7
  ♡ J 9 5 2                   ♡ Q 10 8
  ◇ J 4       W       E       ◇ Q 6 5
  ♣ Q J 10 9 8     S          ♣ K 7
              ♠ A K 5
              ♡ A K 7 6
              ◇ K 10 2
              ♣ A 5 3
```

South plays in Three No Trumps against the lead of the Queen of Clubs. He holds up his Ace until the third round, then leads a low Diamond, planning to duck the trick into East's hand. West can thwart declarer's plan by putting up the Jack. True, this gives South three tricks in the suit if he next finesses the ten of Diamonds, but he will be one trick short of his contract. Clearly if West plays low on the Diamond lead declarer has no problems.

The same theme can occur in suit play:

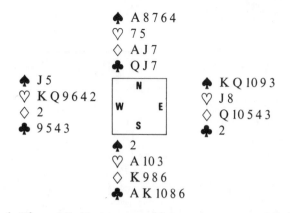

```
              ♠ A 8 7 6 4
              ♡ 7 5
              ◇ A J 7
              ♣ Q J 7
♠ J 5                              ♠ K Q 10 9 3
♡ K Q 9 6 4 2    N                ♡ J 8
◇ 2          W       E            ◇ Q 10 5 4 3
♣ 9 5 4 3        S                ♣ 2
              ♠ 2
              ♡ A 10 3
              ◇ K 9 8 6
              ♣ A K 10 8 6
```

Although Three No Trumps would have been a straightforward affair, South ended in Five Clubs and West led his singleton Diamond. Dummy played low and the ten went to South's King. There were nine tricks in sight; the Diamonds would eventually yield a tenth, but the eleventh had to come from a Heart ruff. With the idea of keeping East out of the lead, South crossed to the table with the Queen of Clubs and led a Heart, planning to put in the ten. However, East went in with the Jack and declarer was forced to win. He made a good try by leading the ten of Hearts from hand, for only West could win this trick, but after a trump had come back South found that the 4–1 trump break was more than he could cope with. After winning in hand and ruffing his last Heart, he could get back to hand only by ruffing a Spade. Eventually the defenders came to a Diamond and a trump for a one-trick defeat.

It is worth noting what happens if East fails to put up the Jack of Hearts. Declarer inserts the ten, and with one more entry to hand is in great comfort.

The next hand is one on which a good player missed an opportunity in defence—not a subtle squeeze-breaking play, but the sort of play that causes you to say afterwards, "Why didn't I think of that?"

At game-all East dealt and opened Three Diamonds. As it was rubber bridge, South, unwisely perhaps, allowed himself to be influenced by 150 for honours and bid Four Hearts. (Whatever

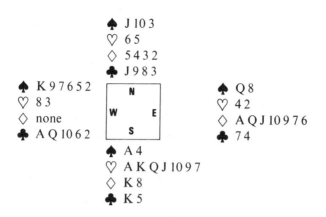

♠ J 10 3
♡ 6 5
◇ 5 4 3 2
♣ J 9 8 3

♠ K 9 7 6 5 2
♡ 8 3
◇ none
♣ A Q 10 6 2

N
W E
S

♠ Q 8
♡ 4 2
◇ A Q J 10 9 7 6
♣ 7 4

♠ A 4
♡ A K Q J 10 9 7
◇ K 8
♣ K 5

the form of scoring, nothing would persuade me to bid anything other than Three No Trumps.) West brooded for some time but passed and Four Hearts became the final contract.

The opening lead was a small trump and from the bidding and West's failure to lead a Diamond South could judge the situation in the suit. There were apparently four losers at least, for although the King of Diamonds was a likely trick there was no entry to dummy. Nevertheless, there was a good chance of forcing West to give dummy the lead, so South drew trumps in two rounds and followed with the King of Clubs. West won with the Ace and cashed the Queen, but now found himself in difficulties. Another Club would allow dummy to win and play a Diamond (even if declarer did not finesse the nine of Clubs for his tenth trick), so West switched to a low Spade. Now South could see daylight. He played the ten of Spades from the table and won East's Queen with the Ace. Another Spade lead finished West off, for he was now bound to concede the lead—and two tricks—to dummy.

East made consoling noises, but his partner had missed the point of the defence. When West is left on lead with the Queen of Clubs he must exit with the King of Spades, not a low Spade. If South takes this trick it is East who wins the next Spade and can cash the Ace of Diamonds, whereas if South ducks, the defence simply plays another Spade to leave the lead in South's hand. Another one that got away!

Do you listen to the bidding? All of it, that is, and not just the final contract? Note how a shrewd defender was able to take full advantage of an over-informative auction on this deal:

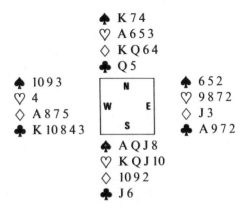

```
              ♠ K 7 4
              ♡ A 6 5 3
              ◇ K Q 6 4
              ♣ Q 5
♠ 10 9 3                      ♠ 6 5 2
♡ 4            N              ♡ 9 8 7 2
◇ A 8 7 5   W     E           ◇ J 3
♣ K 10 8 4 3      S           ♣ A 9 7 2
              ♠ A Q J 8
              ♡ K Q J 10
              ◇ 10 9 2
              ♣ J 6
```

At the first table North–South explored in the scientific manner:

South	North
1 ♠	2 ◇
2 ♡	3 ♣
3 ◇	4 ♡
pass	

North regarded his hand as too good for a simple raise to Four Hearts on the second round and decided to precede it with the "fourth-suit" bid of Three Clubs to show extra strength. This had the unfortunate effect of forcing South to show his tolerance for Diamonds and this proved a decisive factor in the play. West led the four of Clubs to his partner's Ace and won the Club return with his King. Then he switched to a low Diamond (a play he knew could not cost after South's Diamond preference) and dummy's King won. Two rounds of trumps exposed the bad break and now South found himself in trouble. If he drew trumps before playing another Diamond he would be wide open in Clubs, and if, as he did, he tried another Diamond first, East would score a ruff.

At the other table a more direct approach (One Heart—Four Hearts) paid dividends. As before, the defenders cashed two Clubs, when West switched to the ten of Spades. South won and led the two of Diamonds from hand before touching trumps. A duck by West defeats the game as before, but not unreasonably he feared a singleton Diamond in South's hand and hoped for a possible trump trick in East's hand. So he went in with the Ace of Diamonds, and all South's problems were solved.

9
Famous Hands from the Past: 1

I suppose I should make some excuse for including this and the next chapter, for undoubtedly some of the material will be more than familiar to any keen student of bridge literature. However, I found re-reading the hands so stimulating that I'm sure even the knowledgeable player will similarly enjoy them.

A worthy starter is this example from the long records of Oswald Jacoby, who in 1934 took part in the famous Culbertson–Lenz match. In a rubber-bridge game the cards fell as follows:

```
                    ♠ Q J 7 4 3
                    ♡ 9 5
                    ◇ none
                    ♣ K Q J 10 9 2
     ♠ none            N          ♠ 10 8 5 2
     ♡ A K Q J 10 8 3           ♡ 6 4
     ◇ A K Q 10 8 4  W     E    ◇ J 9 5 3
     ♣ none              S        ♣ 8 6 3
                    ♠ A K 9 6
                    ♡ 7 2
                    ◇ 7 6 2
                    ♣ A 7 5 4
```

North was the dealer at love-all and Jacoby sat South. The bidding went:

South	West	North	East
		pass	pass
1 ♠	dble	4 ♠	pass
pass	5 ♡	5 ♠	pass
pass	6 ♡	pass	pass
dble	redble	pass	pass
6 ♠	7 ♡	pass	pass
7 ♠	dble	pass	pass
pass			

West's bidding was a strange mixture of cunning and cupidity. After two tactical underbids he could not resist the temptation to redouble Six Hearts, doubtless reflecting that if this drove the opponents to Six Spades he would eventually buy the contract in Seven Hearts. But by this time he had tipped his hand and Jacoby, suspecting thirteen red cards, decided to sacrifice in Seven Spades.

But it turned out not to be a sacrifice at all, for he made the grand slam! When West brought out his secret weapon, the Ace of Diamonds, Jacoby ruffed high in dummy, led the three of Spades and finessed the six! He then trumped a Diamond low in dummy and finessed the nine of Spades. A third Diamond was ruffed with dummy's last trump and declarer returned to hand with a Club to draw the remaining trumps. Dummy's Clubs then took the rest of the tricks.

If you examine the hand closely you will find that all of Jacoby's manœuvres were essential. If he ruffs the first Diamond with a low trump, then, however he continues, timely interpolation by East of the eight or ten of Spades will destroy the entry situation.

The next deal was taken from the World Par Contest Olympiad of 1963. Par contests tend to be a wearisome collection of advanced technical plays, but there is a touch of genius about this example:

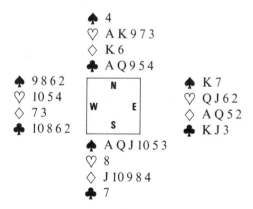

```
              ♠ 4
              ♡ A K 9 7 3
              ◇ K 6
              ♣ A Q 9 5 4
  ♠ 9 8 6 2        N        ♠ K 7
  ♡ 10 5 4                  ♡ Q J 6 2
  ◇ 7 3      W        E     ◇ A Q 5 2
  ♣ 10 8 6 2       S        ♣ K J 3
              ♠ A Q J 10 5 3
              ♡ 8
              ◇ J 10 9 8 4
              ♣ 7
```

East deals at game-all and opens One No Trump which South over-calls with Two Spades. After a pass by West, North has an awkward bid. Probably Three No Trumps, the "official" recommendation, is as good as anything. East passes and South converts to Four Spades. The seven of Diamonds is the directed lead. It is easy to see how the play would go at the table. East cashes two Diamond winners and, as there are no prospects in Hearts or Clubs, tries a third Diamond. West ruffs with the six in front of dummy, but later South picks up the King of Spades by a finesse and makes his contract. On to the next deal. . . .

But in a par contest you have to think up something more subtle. Can you see any other possible defence?

If West is very alert indeed he may work out that the only hope is for his partner to win an early trump trick and give him another Diamond ruff. That will be simple if partner has the Ace of Spades —indeed the contract will go two off—but suppose he has only K x in Spades?

I can see you're getting there. West blandly ruffs the third Diamond with the *two* of Spades, permitting dummy to over-ruff with the four. Then East wins the second round of trumps and leads a fourth Diamond for West to ruff.

However, that is not the end of the story, for South should resist the bait. He allows West's two of Spades to hold the trick and thereafter cannot be stopped from making the contract.

Although an engaging exercise, this is not really an ideal par hand. So few Wests will ruff with the two of Spades that almost all declarers will obtain their par award without working for it.

Having started this chapter with a hand from the Culberston–Lenz rubber-bridge match, I feel that I ought to include two more. The match, which began in December 1931 and lasted a month, was billed as a test between the "official" system of Sydney Lenz, in which opening bids of one, two and three showed increasing strength, and Culbertson's approach forcing method.

Culbertson played with four different partners, mostly his wife and Lightner. Lenz intended to play throughout with Oswald Jacoby, but after about 100 rubbers, two-thirds of the match, Jacoby resigned in dramatic circumstances and a Commander Liggett made a brief appearance on the scene of history.

System apart, Lenz had exasperated his partner by several poor bids, of which this was a horrific example:

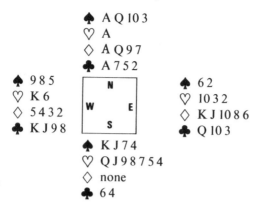

♠ A Q 10 3
♡ A
♢ A Q 9 7
♣ A 7 5 2

♠ 9 8 5
♡ K 6
♢ 5 4 3 2
♣ K J 9 8

♠ 6 2
♡ 10 3 2
♢ K J 10 8 6
♣ Q 10 3

♠ K J 7 4
♡ Q J 9 8 7 5 4
♢ none
♣ 6 4

South dealt at game-all and this was the bidding:

South (Jacoby)	West (Culbertson)	North (Lenz)	East (Lightner)
1 ♡	pass	3 NT	pass
4 ♡	pass	4 NT	pass
5 ♡	pass	6 NT	pass
pass	dble	pass	pass
7 ♡	dble	pass	pass
pass			

Lenz maintained that he was not beguiled by his aces but could be confident of making Six No Trumps opposite any "proper" vulnerable opening. Against that, Jacoby was famous for his psychic and semi-psychic bids.

Culbertson patted himself on the back for a shrewd psychological stroke in doubling Six No Trumps. It is true that East must find a Club lead to beat this. On the other hand, Seven Hearts would have been possible if North had held a second trump; and of course it is clear that Seven Spades is in the bag on any lead. Say a Club is led; North wins with the Ace and the Ace of Hearts is then cashed. Then South draws trumps having first ruffed a Heart in dummy and discarded his losing Club on the Ace of Diamonds.

It would be wrong to judge the general standard of slam bidding from this example. On the whole, the players sustained very well the lack of all modern conventions.

The other hand from the match had historical as well as technical interest, for according to the referee, Lt. (now General) Gruenther, it precipitated the break between Lenz and Jacoby:

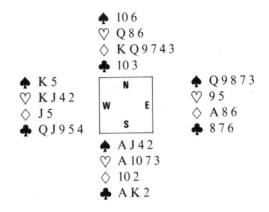

```
                      ♠ 10 6
                      ♡ Q 8 6
                      ◇ K Q 9 7 4 3
                      ♣ 10 3
   ♠ K 5                                ♠ Q 9 8 7 3
   ♡ K J 4 2           N                ♡ 9 5
   ◇ J 5            W     E             ◇ A 8 6
   ♣ Q J 9 5 4         S                ♣ 8 7 6
                      ♠ A J 4 2
                      ♡ A 10 7 3
                      ◇ 10 2
                      ♣ A K 2
```

It was game-all and North–South had 35 below the line. The bidding went:

South (Culbertson)	West (Lenz)	North (Mrs Culbertson)	East (Jacoby)
1 ♠	pass	2 ◇	pass
2 NT	pass	pass	pass

As each trick in No Trumps counted for 35 in those days, this was a game contract. Lenz led the Queen of Clubs, Jacoby played the seven, and South ducked. West continued with the Jack of Clubs, on which East played the eight and South the Ace. Declarer led a Diamond to the Queen, which held, then came back to hand with the Ace of Hearts and led another Diamond, won by East's Ace.

Most players in East's position would have battled on with Clubs now, but Jacoby realized that declarer was going to get to dummy eventually with the Queen of Hearts and meanwhile three Clubs, a Heart and a Diamond would not be enough to beat the contract. A Spade trick was required and he now led the three of

Spades, a fine play. Culbertson should perhaps have gone up with the Ace, but he played low and West won with the King.

If Lenz had reverted to Clubs now, the contract could have been beaten. Unfortunately, Jacoby's rather pointless false-carding in Clubs had persuaded Lenz that Culbertson had K 6 against his own 9 5 4. He returned a Spade and declarer made an overtrick.

"Needless to say," reports Gruenther, "there were recriminations. . . . Mr Jacoby, incidentally, said he had made a play that only twelve experts in the country would understand. And unfortunately, he commented, Mr Lenz did not seem, at that particular moment anyway, to be among the vaunted 12." At the end of this session the partnership broke up.

One of the luckiest slams ever made in a World Championship came along in the Italy–US match in 1959. The deal, on analysis, seemed to be a death-trap for North–South:

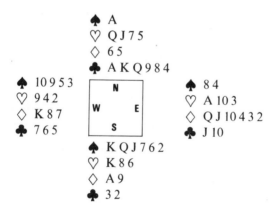

East was the dealer at game-all. Playing with Clubs or Spades as trumps, declarer appears to have abundant tricks—thirteen without a Heart lead—but after a Diamond opening there is an unfortunate and insuperable block in either contract. The American audience watching Bridgerama—an electrified board for presenting all four hands, the bidding and the play, to a large audience—was much relieved when Fishbein and Hazen stopped short with this auction:

South	North
1 ♠	2 ♣
2 ♠	3 ♡
3 ♠	4 ♠
pass	

Both players had something in reserve but one cannot say that any of the bids were wrong. West led a Diamond and South made eleven tricks for a score of 450.

At the other table the American East, playing weak two-bids, opened with Two Diamonds. The bidding went like this:

South (Belladonna)	West	North (Avarelli)	East
			2 ♢
dble	pass	3 ♢	pass
3 ♠	pass	4 ♣	pass
4 ♡ (!)	pass	5 ♢	pass
5 NT	pass	6 ♡	pass
pass	pass		

Avarelli's Three Diamond bid announced a good hand (which he certainly had). Belladonna might perhaps have jumped to Four Spades at this point, to get it off his chest that he had a good suit and good values. When his partner bid Four Clubs over Three Spades Belladonna bid an imaginative Four Hearts, perhaps thinking that if his partner lacked Spade support he would have Heart length. Avarelli took the Heart bid seriously and asked about Diamond control. Five No Trumps showed the Ace and Averelli then bid Six Hearts. So there they were in the worst of three suits, but the contract proved to be unbeatable!

Belladonna won the Diamond lead, cashed the Ace of Spades and led off Ace, King, Queen of Clubs. To prevent a Diamond discard, East ruffed the third Club with the ten of Hearts. South over-ruffed, discarded a Diamond from dummy on the King of Spades, then led the eight of Hearts and ran it. Finis.

Although it hurts me slightly to reproduce the following deal, for reasons which will become rapidly apparent, it has considerable instructional value. It occurred in a Gold Cup match and featured what my partner used to describe whimsically as one of my rare mistakes.

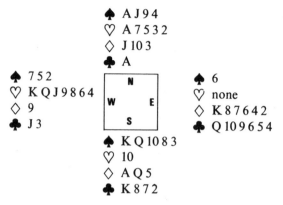

```
              ♠ A J 9 4
              ♡ A 7 5 3 2
              ◇ J 10 3
              ♣ A
  ♠ 7 5 2          N          ♠ 6
  ♡ K Q J 9 8 6 4             ♡ none
  ◇ 9         W       E       ◇ K 8 7 6 4 2
  ♣ J 3            S          ♣ Q 10 9 6 5 4
              ♠ K Q 10 8 3
              ♡ 10
              ◇ A Q 5
              ♣ K 8 7 2
```

South was the dealer and at love-all the bidding at my table went:

South	West	North	East
1 ♠	2 ♡	3 ♡	pass
3 ♠	pass	6 ♠	pass
pass	pass		

The King of Hearts was led and dummy's Ace ruffed. East returned a Diamond and, as South, I had to let this run. When dummy's ten took the trick I thought I was home. Intending to ruff two Clubs I cashed the Ace and came to hand with a trump. After a Club ruff and another round of trumps this was the position:

```
              ♠ J
              ♡ 7 5 3 2
              ◇ J 3
              ♣ none
  ♠ 7              N          ♠ none
  ♡ Q J 9 8 6 4             ♡ none
  ◇ none      W       E       ◇ K 8 7 4
  ♣ none           S          ♣ Q 10 9
              ♠ K 10 3
              ♡ none
              ◇ A Q
              ♣ K 8
```

After ruffing one more Club I still needed the Diamond finesse and West made his last trump. The play to the first two tricks was fraught with emotion and this may have caused me to take my eye off the ball. Instead of trying to ruff two Clubs in dummy I should have ruffed three Hearts in hand, reversing the dummy. Nothing could have gone wrong then.

I was lucky in one sense. My team-mates at the other table were not well placed to rebuke me for failing to make Six Spades, for there the bidding went:

South	West	North	East
1 ♠	2 ♡	3 ♡	4 NT
dble	5 ♡	dble	6 ♣
dble	pass	pass	pass

This was six down, for a loss of 1100. In my opinion, East was wrong to take command in this way when it was likely that the opponents would be running into freakish distribution.

I seem to be hopping around with my choice of hands, but another deal from the 1934 Culbertson–Lenz match came to mind soon afterwards. Most of the interesting hands from that match were discussed by the Culbertsons, by Jacoby and the referee, but for some reason only Jacoby had anything to say about this one:

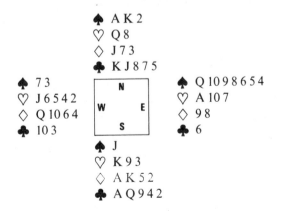

It was the first hand of the twentieth rubber and the bidding went:

South	West	North	East
(Jacoby)	(Culbertson)	(Lenz)	(Mrs Culbertson)
			pass
1 ♣	pass	3 ♣	3 ♠
4 ♠	pass	5 ♣	pass
6 ♣	pass	pass	pass

Jacoby's comment reads as follows:

This was a very lucky hand for us. After Mr Lenz's jump response to my own One Club bid and Mrs Culbertson's Spade bid, I arbitrarily decided to contract for a slam, but to camouflage the bidding by first showing an apparently void Spade suit in the hope that I would obtain a Diamond or a Heart lead which I felt would be more favourable.

As the hand actually stood, the normal Spade or Club lead by Mr Culbertson would have caused us to go one down. If Mr Lenz had held two Diamonds and three Hearts the slam would have been a lay-down against any lead.

Mrs Culbertson led the Ace of Hearts out of turn, and I now called a Diamond from Mr Culbertson. The play of the Jack from dummy gave me the hand without any difficulty. It may be noted that my calling the Diamond lead made the penalty of real value.

Apart from the old-world courtesy which rather dates it, what strikes you about this little piece?

For one thing, you cannot nowadays call for a specified suit after a lead out of turn. (You may debar a Heart lead, or treat the Ace of Hearts as an exposed card, or accept the lead.) Anything else?

Well, suppose a Spade or a Club had been led. I dare say Jacoby would have found the winning line. After drawing trumps declarer leads a low Heart from the table. East must duck, as otherwise a Diamond from dummy will be discarded on the King of Hearts.

Declarer now crosses to dummy, discards a Heart on the second Spade and cashes the A K of Diamonds, expecting East to be short of this suit. Then he exits with a Heart to the Ace and East is obliged to concede a ruff and discard.

It is an attractive example of avoidance play (ducking under the Ace of Hearts) combined with elimination.

Turning to more modern times, here is a hand that was played in a World Championship match between Italy and France. It occurred during a spell when France gained 53 match points in four boards. You may think that the French were lucky on this occasion:

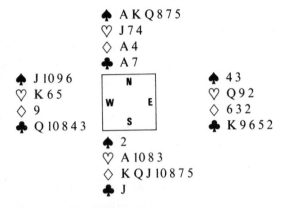

```
              ♠ A K Q 8 7 5
              ♡ J 7 4
              ◇ A 4
              ♣ A 7
♠ J 10 9 6          N          ♠ 4 3
♡ K 6 5                        ♡ Q 9 2
◇ 9          W         E       ◇ 6 3 2
♣ Q 10 8 4 3       S           ♣ K 9 6 5 2
              ♠ 2
              ♡ A 10 8 3
              ◇ K Q J 10 8 7 5
              ♣ J
```

East was the dealer and East–West were vulnerable. This was the bidding when Italy were North–South:

South (Chiaradia)	West (Théron)	North (Garozzo)	East (Desrousseaux)
			pass
1 ♡	pass	2 ♠	pass
3 ◇	pass	3 ♠	pass
4 NT	pass	5 ♠	pass
5 NT	pass	6 ◇	pass
7 ◇	pass	pass	pass

The grand slam would have been easy if Théron had not made the good lead of a Club. He knew that declarer would need to ruff a Spade to establish the suit and hoped that the Club lead would drive out an important entry.

Two fairly obvious lines of play suggest themselves. One is to cash the Ace of Spades and ruff a Spade, then hope that the trumps will be 2–2 (in itself a better chance than to find the

126

Spades 3–3). The other possibility is to play out all the trumps, winning if the Spades are 3–3 or if the player with the long Spades holds the King and Queen of Hearts.

Chiaradia played for the first line and was defeated when the Diamonds broke 3–1. It looks on the surface as though the squeeze would fail too, but if Chiaradia had played out all the trumps he would probably have stumbled on the winning solution. This is the position after the Ace of Clubs and five rounds of Diamonds.

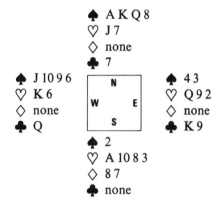

On the eight of Diamonds West can afford a Heart, and the Jack of Hearts is thrown from dummy. When the last trump is led West must keep the King of Hearts to protect his partner from the finesse, so must release the Queen of Clubs. Now dummy throws a Spade and on three rounds of Spades East is squeezed in Hearts and Clubs. It is a type of play known as a "guard squeeze".

At the other table the French South opened with a transfer bid of Three Clubs. Nervous lest Three Diamonds be passed, North jumped to Four Spades, where they rested. This inglorious display at least resulted in a plus score.

As I observed at the start of this chapter, many of the deals have become well known. However, the next hand is unlikely to be familiar, played as it was by a young Norwegian in 1935. It is strange that the theme does not occur more often. Perhaps it does, unnoticed.

South opened One Diamond and, after ascertaining that his partner held the King of Diamonds and two aces, North propelled his

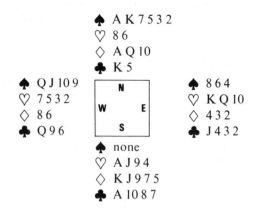

♠ A K 7 5 3 2
♥ 8 6
◇ A Q 10
♣ K 5

♠ Q J 10 9   ♠ 8 6 4
♥ 7 5 3 2   ♥ K Q 10
◇ 8 6   ◇ 4 3 2
♣ Q 9 6   ♣ J 4 3 2

♠ none
♥ A J 9 4
◇ K J 9 7 5
♣ A 10 8 7

side into Seven Diamonds. West led the Queen of Spades and it was clear that the Spades had to be established. South ruffed the opening lead, crossed to the Queen of Diamonds, and ruffed another Spade. After a second round of trumps the position was:

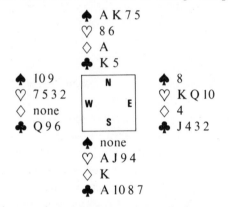

♠ A K 7 5
♥ 8 6
◇ A
♣ K 5

♠ 10 9   ♠ 8
♥ 7 5 3 2   ♥ K Q 10
◇ none   ◇ 4
♣ Q 9 6   ♣ J 4 3 2

♠ none
♥ A J 9 4
◇ K
♣ A 10 8 7

You will observe that if declarer draws the last trump and plays off the Spades he cannot exert sufficient pressure. East discards two Clubs and a Heart and West can take care of the Clubs.

The declarer found a neat solution by leaving the low trump at large. In the diagram position he led off the Ace and King of Spades. East ruffed (he may delay the ruff, but it makes no difference) and South over-ruffed. Then he returned to the King of Clubs and played off the remaining Spades, forcing East to let go a Club. Three rounds of Clubs followed, dummy ruffing, and South's fourth Club provided the thirteenth trick.

You may wonder, where did the extra trick come from? The

answer is that the Spade winner lost when East ruffed was recovered because the two trumps were made separately; and the Ace of Diamonds became free for the ruff of the third round of Clubs, to the embarrassment of East. In a sense the Ace of Diamonds could always be used for the ruff, but there were entry problems.

I met the following problem hand one year when I was playing in a European Championship. It proved to be a valuable secret weapon for the Swiss, who claimed that they wore down their opponents by showing them the problem overnight. I find tedious those problems that develop into a complicated end-game; the charm of this one is that it rests on a well-known type of play, and the solution, once you get the idea, is simple.

```
                    ♠ A K 10
                    ♡ A 10 3
                    ◇ K J
                    ♣ K 5 4 3 2
    ♠ Q J 9 8 7 6    ┌─────────┐    ♠ 4 3 2
    ♡ K              │    N    │    ♡ Q J 9 8 7
    ◇ Q              │ W     E │    ◇ 10 8 3 2
    ♣ Q 10 9 8 7     │    S    │    ♣ J
                     └─────────┘
                    ♠ 5
                    ♡ 6 5 4 2
                    ◇ A 9 7 6 5 4
                    ♣ A 6
```

South has to make Five Diamonds against the lead of the Queen of Spades. There are ten tricks in view—five Diamonds, two Spades, two Clubs and a Heart. One's first thought is to develop a squeeze against West in the black suits. Suppose you win with the King of Spades, cash the King and Jack of Diamonds, enter hand with a Club and give East his trump trick? East exits with a Heart and the squeeze won't work because if you play King and another Club to get back to hand you lose touch with the dummy.

So you wonder next whether you can end-play East and force him to lead up to dummy's A 10 of Spades. Or perhaps you can throw West in with a Club and make him lead a Spade? Again you are frustrated by the lack of entries.

You might spend the next two hours looking for some unusual trump coup combined with a squeeze. Such endings do exist, but not on this hand.

Now consider a different possibility altogether—a dummy reversal! You aim to take five ruffs in your hand, taking seven trump tricks altogether. You make a surprising start by cashing the Ace of Spades at trick 2 and discarding the Ace of Clubs. Then you ruff a Spade, lead a Club to the King, and ruff a Club. After a Diamond to the King you ruff one more Club, arriving at this position:

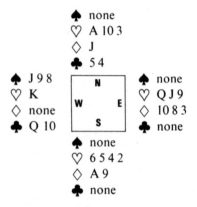

```
                    ♠ none
                    ♡ A 10 3
                    ◇ J
                    ♣ 5 4
      ♠ J 9 8                    ♠ none
      ♡ K          N             ♡ Q J 9
      ◇ none    W     E          ◇ 10 8 3
      ♣ Q 10       S             ♣ none
                    ♠ none
                    ♡ 6 5 4 2
                    ◇ A 9
                    ♣ none
```

Now you let West hold the King of Hearts and make him your accomplice in the trump reduction. He plays a black card and you ruff. You cross to the Ace of Hearts, ruff a Club with the Ace of Diamonds, and the Jack of Diamonds is the eleventh trick.

The next hand from the past was described at the time as "The Earthquake at São Paulo". It occurred in 1961 when a French team on its way to a World Championship in Argentina stopped off to play a challenge match against Brazil. To present the various dramatic features in order: at about two o'clock in the morning, Bacherich, of France, picked up as dealer at game-all:

```
♠ none
♡ A Q 10 9 8 7 6 5 4 3 2
◇ none
♣ K 4
```

Betraying no excitement, he passed. West passed and Deruy, North, opened with a conventional Two Clubs. East over-called with Two Spades. What now? Bacherich shifted gear and bid Seven Hearts. But that was not the end of the auction. First, the four hands:

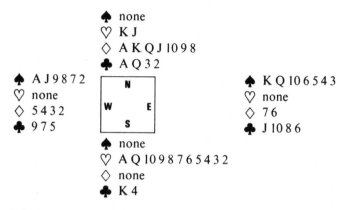

```
                    ♠ none
                    ♡ K J
                    ◇ A K Q J 10 9 8
                    ♣ A Q 3 2
♠ A J 9 8 7 2      ┌─────────┐      ♠ K Q 10 6 5 4 3
♡ none             │    N    │      ♡ none
◇ 5 4 3 2          │ W     E │      ◇ 7 6
♣ 9 7 5            │    S    │      ♣ J 10 8 6
                   └─────────┘
                    ♠ none
                    ♡ A Q 10 9 8 7 6 5 4 3 2
                    ◇ none
                    ♣ K 4
```

And this was the full bidding:

South	West	North	East
pass	pass	2 ♣	2 ♠
7 ♡	pass	pass	7 ♠
pass	pass	7 NT	dble
pass	pass	pass	

The defence made the first seven tricks for a penalty of 2000 points. There was a hidden psychological explanation for North's bid of Seven No Trumps. West had thought awhile before passing Seven Hearts and this, in the opinion of the Frenchmen, should have barred East from sacrificing in Seven Spades. When the Brazilian referee declined to accept this view, Deruy, in the manner of a tennis player who bangs the ball out of court, bid a self-destructive Seven No Trumps.

One of the piquant features of the deal was that whereas one South player passed, the other opened Two Clubs. When the French were East–West the bidding went:

South	West	North	East
2 ♣	2 ♡	3 ◇	pass
3 ♡	pass	4 ◇	pass
4 ♡	pass	4 NT	pass
5 ◇	pass	7 ♡	pass
pass	pass		

West's antediluvian psychic bid of Two Hearts did not assist the partnership to find its sacrifice. East thought about bidding Seven Spades on his own but was not entirely convinced that his opponents were in the right contract.

The swing, in the scale then used, was 29 match points, but the French still won.

Another old hand gives me the opportunity to re-mount one of my favourite hobby-horses—the folly of bidding the "unusual No Trump" when you have little chance of buying the contract.

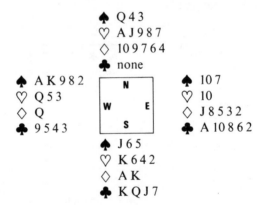

```
              ♠ Q 4 3
              ♡ A J 9 8 7
              ◇ 10 9 7 6 4
              ♣ none
♠ A K 9 8 2      N          ♠ 10 7
♡ Q 5 3                     ♡ 10
◇ Q          W       E      ◇ J 8 5 3 2
♣ 9 5 4 3        S          ♣ A 10 8 6 2
              ♠ J 6 5
              ♡ K 6 4 2
              ◇ A K
              ♣ K Q J 7
```

North dealt with North–South vulnerable and the bidding went:

South	West	North	East
		pass	pass
1 NT	pass	2 ◇	2 NT
3 ♡	pass	4 ♡	pass
pass	dble	pass	pass
pass			

North's Two Diamonds was a transfer bid, requesting South to bid Two Hearts. This emboldened South, the veteran Oswald Jacoby, to make a free bid of Three Hearts over East's intervention. It was just possible, at the score, that East's unusual Two No Trumps might have led to a worthwhile sacrifice, but far more likely that it would assist the opponents to judge the hand well in the play.

One consequence of East's bid was that West appeared to have a good double of Four Hearts. The defence began with three rounds of Spades, East ruffing, and a Diamond was returned to declarer's Ace. After a long appraisal Jacoby led a low Heart, finessing dummy's seven, then cashed the Ace of Hearts, producing this position:

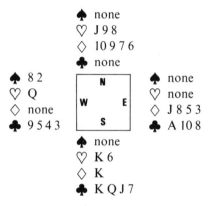

```
              ♠ none
              ♡ J 9 8
              ◇ 10 9 7 6
              ♣ none
  ♠ 8 2          N          ♠ none
  ♡ Q                       ♡ none
  ◇ none     W       E      ◇ J 8 5 3
  ♣ 9 5 4 3      S          ♣ A 10 8
              ♠ none
              ♡ K 6
              ◇ K
              ♣ K Q J 7
```

East was in trouble when South led a third Heart to the King. If he throws a Diamond, South cashes the King, enters dummy and leads the ten of Diamonds, establishing the suit. So East let a Club go and now declarer had time to set up two Club winners.

The declarer's timing had to be exactly right for this unusual ending. He could not possibly have managed it without the aid of East's revealing Two No Trumps.

At one time the same boards were used for both semi-finals of the Gold Cup, allowing fascinating comparisons to be made. It seems rather a pity that this practice is no longer followed. The following deal was played in an event just after the war:

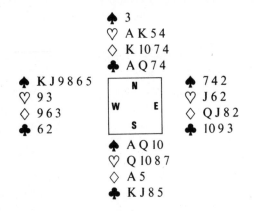

♠ 3
♡ A K 5 4
◇ K 10 7 4
♣ A Q 7 4

♠ K J 9 8 6 5
♡ 9 3
◇ 9 6 3
♣ 6 2

♠ 7 4 2
♡ J 6 2
◇ Q J 8 2
♣ 10 9 3

♠ A Q 10
♡ Q 10 8 7
◇ A 5
♣ K J 8 5

Well, what contract would you like to play in? Seven Hearts, I expect, and quite right too. However, only one North–South pair got there. The other three resting-spots were Six Hearts made with an overtrick, Two Spades redoubled, made with an overtrick, and Six No Trumps one down.

The Two Spades redoubled arose as follows:

South	West	North	East
		1 ♣	pass
2 ♠	dble	redble	pass
pass	pass		

South chose Two Spades because he did not want to force in a suit where he lacked a top honour. West's double was pretty silly, so was North's redouble and South's final pass. South made nine tricks, but that was worth only 790 and did not compensate for the slam at the other table. Playing in Hearts, declarer needed only to take two Spade ruffs in the North hand.

The most interesting play was when South finished in Six No Trumps after West had over-called in Spades (North opened One Club and South responded One Heart). Sitting West, I led the six of Diamonds. My partner contributed the Jack and South won with the Ace. Declarer played off four rounds of Hearts, four of Clubs, then finessed the ten of Diamonds, trying for his twelfth trick. My partner won and we made a Spade to defeat the contract. In view of the Spade over-call South should look for an end-play. It is essential to keep an entry to hand after the Club and Heart

134

winners have been played. In other words, declarer must go up with the King of Diamonds at trick 1. Then he reaches this position:

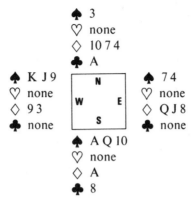

```
              ♠ 3
              ♡ none
              ◇ 10 7 4
              ♣ A
  ♠ K J 9              ♠ 7 4
  ♡ none      N        ♡ none
  ◇ 9 3   W       E    ◇ Q J 8
  ♣ none       S       ♣ none
              ♠ A Q 10
              ♡ none
              ◇ A
              ♣ 8
```

Now if West discards a Spade on the last Club South can set up a Spade winner; and if West discards a Diamond South cashes the Ace of Diamonds and exits with the Queen of Spades.

It goes without saying that partners should not discuss a hand while it is in progress, and this applies especially to the defenders. However, we all know that in some games, the chatty ones, the rule is broken all the time. This occasionally happens even in tournament play. A celebrated example occurred at my table during an early round of the Gold Cup a number of years ago:

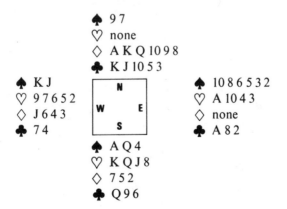

```
              ♠ 9 7
              ♡ none
              ◇ A K Q 10 9 8
              ♣ K J 10 5 3
  ♠ K J                ♠ 10 8 6 5 3 2
  ♡ 9 7 6 5 2   N      ♡ A 10 4 3
  ◇ J 6 4 3  W     E   ◇ none
  ♣ 7 4         S      ♣ A 8 2
              ♠ A Q 4
              ♡ K Q J 8
              ◇ 7 5 2
              ♣ Q 9 6
```

South was the dealer at game-all. My partner, who was South, chose to open with an approach bid of One Club. He was under strength for a vulnerable No Trump and there were objections to opening One Heart. The bid of One Club let loose a brief storm:

South	West	North	East
1 ♣	pass	6 ♣	dble
pass	pass	pass	

I might have bid the North hand more scientifically, of course, but there are times when speed is more important than accuracy. This type of contract so often depends on the lead that I wanted·to give the opponents a blind guess. Perhaps that wasn't a bad idea, for after learned reflection West selected the King of Spades as his opening move. My partner won and led a trump. The King lost to the Ace and a Spade came back. East almost fell out of his chair when South took the trick with the Queen. The Queen of Clubs followed and at this point East could contain himself no longer.

"That was a brilliant lead," he said bitterly. "Lead a Diamond or a Heart and we beat it easily."

Now even if the Diamonds were solid there would be only eleven tricks after a Diamond lead, but was East in the mood for that sort of accounting? It seemed more likely that a Diamond void was grinding at his soul. After drawing the last trump South led a Diamond and put in dummy's eight on the first round. I'm glad to say that he didn't forget to compliment me on my bidding.

In the qualifying round of the 1964 Olympiad played in New York,

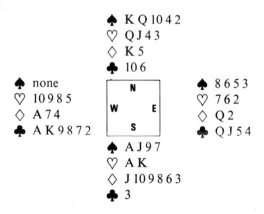

```
              ♠ K Q 10 4 2
              ♡ Q J 4 3
              ◇ K 5
              ♣ 10 6
  ♠ none         N          ♠ 8 6 5 3
  ♡ 10 9 8 5                ♡ 7 6 2
  ◇ A 7 4     W       E     ◇ Q 2
  ♣ A K 9 8 7 2    S        ♣ Q J 5 4
              ♠ A J 9 7
              ♡ A K
              ◇ J 10 9 8 6 3
              ♣ 3
```

there were short matches of eighteen boards and inevitably some surprises. The hand opposite features the first giant-killing performance by Chinese players in this type of event. I shall never forget the excitement (not to say amusement) when the news spread that the Republic of China (Formosa) had beaten the USA 7–0.

East was the dealer and North–South were vulnerable. This was the bidding when the Americans held the East–West cards:

South (Wu)	West (Robinson)	North (Wong)	East (Jordan)
			pass
1 ◇	2 ♣	2 ♠	5 ♣
5 ♠	pass	6 ♠	pass
pass	7 ♣	dble	pass
pass	pass		

East's Five Clubs was a typical advance sacrifice, but he was out-manœuvred by North. Holding no Ace, North had no reason to suppose that Six Spades would be on, but he also knew that non-vulnerable opponents would be very loth to risk a slam being made against them. The defenders took the maximum. After ruffing the Spade lead and drawing trumps, West led the ten of Hearts. South cashed the Ace and King before exiting with a Diamond. Thus North–South gained 700 points, which was better than playing in Six Spades with two Aces missing.

At the other table the American North–South pair doubled their opponents in Five Clubs. As before, West ruffed the Spade lead, drew trumps and led a Heart. South won and switched to the Jack of Diamonds. Now the Hearts were blocked and West was only one down. This gave Formosa a swing of 600, which counted as 12 match points.

Two of the more colourful teams in the European Championships are Spain and Lebanon. The next hand is drawn from one of their past encounters:

137

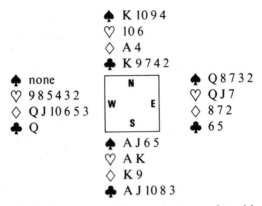

```
              ♠ K 10 9 4
              ♡ 10 6
              ◇ A 4
              ♣ K 9 7 4 2
♠ none                    N              ♠ Q 8 7 3 2
♡ 9 8 5 4 3 2      W          E          ♡ Q J 7
◇ Q J 10 6 5 3                           ◇ 8 7 2
♣ Q                       S              ♣ 6 5
              ♠ A J 6 5
              ♡ A K
              ◇ K 9
              ♣ A J 10 8 3
```

South was the dealer and North–South were vulnerable. This was the bidding when Spain held the North–South cards:

South	West	North	East
1 ♣	5 ◇	dble	pass
5 ♠	pass	6 ♠	pass
pass	pass		

West's enterprising leap to Five Diamonds would have deterred some opponents, but South was determined not to be robbed of a vulnerable slam. Six Spades proved easy to make in spite of the trump break. The declarer won the Heart lead and simply drew four rounds of trumps, leaving the defence to make the Queen of Spades.

The entertainment at the other table was much more startling:

South	West	North	East
2 NT	3 ♡	4 ♡	dble
redble	4 ♠	4 NT	pass
5 ♠	pass	6 ♣	6 ♠
7 ♣	pass	pass	pass
dble	pass	pass	pass

The bidding was normal up to West's Four Spades. This, presumably, was designed to suggest a line of defence should East be able to win the first trick in a Club contract. However, East concluded somewhat improbably that the Spade bid was a genuine suit; even so, he could have bid Seven Hearts over Seven Clubs, giving his partner the option.

The strangest part of all is that, according to the records, West, playing Seven Spades doubled, somehow made six tricks. The defenders must have cashed their winners in the red suits and drawn too many trumps. Losing 1300 at this table, Spain won the board, having registered 1430 for the Spade slam that made.

10
Famous Hands from the Past: 2

Bidding misunderstandings are usually costly affairs, but a hand from the European Championship at Vienna in 1957 proved that this is not always the case. When Texas responses to One No Trump were first introduced, Four Diamonds invited a transfer to Four Hearts and Four Hearts a transfer to Four Spades. That method had its hazards, as this deal from our match against Iceland illustrates.

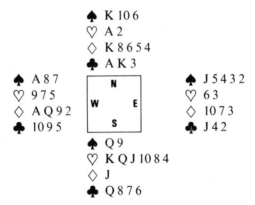

```
              ♠ K 10 6
              ♡ A 2
              ◊ K 8 6 5 4
              ♣ A K 3
    ♠ A 8 7        N         ♠ J 5 4 3 2
    ♡ 9 7 5                  ♡ 6 3
    ◊ A Q 9 2   W     E      ◊ 10 7 3
    ♣ 10 9 5        S        ♣ J 4 2
              ♠ Q 9
              ♡ K Q J 10 8 4
              ◊ J
              ♣ Q 8 7 6
```

North was the dealer at game-all. My partner, Terence Reese, opened with One No Trump. East passed and I bid Four Hearts. I had, of course, forgotten that this requested a transfer to Four Spades. Having had one or two similar misadventures in the past, we had agreed on a fine of 100 Austrian schillings for any player who forgot the convention. When North bid Four Spades, I realized my mistake and jumped to Six Hearts. I wasn't worth this bid but I wanted to make sure of playing in the right strain.

Six Hearts was passed out and I avoided my partner's eye when West led the Ace of Spades and dummy went down. But the miracle happened: West continued with a second Spade, enabling

140

me to discard my Diamond loser in due course on the King of Spades. On top of that, the Clubs broke evenly. Grimly, I handed over 100 Austrian schillings.

The Icemen for once almost lost their cool, as the phrase goes. "I thought he must have a void to bid six without an ace," West explained to his partner and the world at large.

From this time on we switched to "South African Texas", wherein Four Diamonds asks for Four Spades, Four Clubs for Four Hearts. As these responses (unlike Four Hearts) are unusual, one is less prone to forgetfulness.

I may have been a little lucky on the previous deal, but there was no room for slackness in defence on this hand. Indeed, it was a rare spectacle—two impossible game contracts were allowed to make in World Championship play.

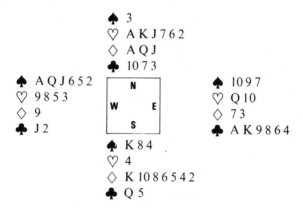

```
                    ♠ 3
                    ♡ A K J 7 6 2
                    ◇ A Q J
                    ♣ 10 7 3
    ♠ A Q J 6 5 2      N        ♠ 10 9 7
    ♡ 9 8 5 3                   ♡ Q 10
    ◇ 9          W       E      ◇ 7 3
    ♣ J 2                       ♣ A K 9 8 6 4
                     S
                    ♠ K 8 4
                    ♡ 4
                    ◇ K 10 8 6 5 4 2
                    ♣ Q 5
```

West was the dealer at love-all. This was the bidding when the Americans were North–South:

South	West	North	East
	pass	1 ♡	pass
2 ◇	pass	3 ♠	pass
4 ◇	pass	4 ♡	pass
5 ◇	pass	pass	pass

North's Three Spades was a so-called "fragment bid", showing Diamond support and short Spades.

The defence began with two top Clubs and then East, instead of shifting to a Spade, led a third Club, allowing the declarer to dispose of his Spade losers on dummy's Hearts. This was extremely poor play by East for two reasons: (1) there was no prospect of establishing a trump trick for West, and (2) it was clear from South's failure to bid Four Spades over Four Hearts that he did not hold the Ace of Spades.

At the other table the bidding went:

South	West	North	East
	pass	1 ♡	pass
2 ◇	2 ♠	3 ◇	3 ♠
3 NT	pass	pass	pass

West chose to lead a Heart, enabling South to run like a bunny for ten tricks—instead of four down on a Club lead. A Club was the obvious choice because it was unlikely that South would be able to run nine tricks without playing on Hearts, the suit bid by North; no need, therefore, to lead a Heart.

There was considerable scope for gain on this deal from the 1957 trials; one team had the chance of making game in both rooms. However, both declarers missed the winning lines of play and their team lost points all round.

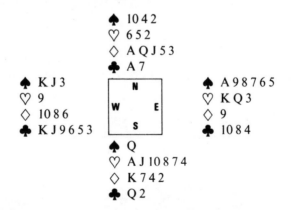

```
            ♠ 10 4 2
            ♡ 6 5 2
            ◇ A Q J 5 3
            ♣ A 7
♠ K J 3          N          ♠ A 9 8 7 6 5
♡ 9                         ♡ K Q 3
◇ 10 8 6    W       E       ◇ 9
♣ K J 9 6 5 3    S          ♣ 10 8 4
            ♠ Q
            ♡ A J 10 8 7 4
            ◇ K 7 4 2
            ♣ Q 2
```

East dealt at game-all and at one table elected to open One Spade. South cautiously passed but, when West's raise to Two Spades

142

came round to him, contested with Two No Trumps (a curious choice). West showed his Clubs, North his Diamonds, and now East–West bid on to Four Spades. Affronted, North doubled and South led the two of Diamonds. North won and declarer ruffed the Diamond continuation. As can be seen, the cards lie favourably but East mis-guessed the Clubs to go one down. After South's initial pass and North's final double, this was one that he should perhaps have got right.

At the other table East passed and South opened One Heart. In spite of an over-call by East, South was allowed to play in Four Hearts and West led the three of Spades. East won with the Ace and switched to his singleton Diamond. There was a clear danger of a Diamond ruff and South tried to meet it by playing Ace and another trump. East won the second trump and returned a Club to establish a fourth trick for the defence.

Curiously enough, South would almost welcome a ruff. If he wins the Diamond switch in dummy and finesses the ten of Hearts he certainly succeeds as the cards lie, but suppose West can win and give his partner a ruff. South can win the Club return, draw the last trump, and safely discard his Club on dummy's long Diamond.

What are your reactions to an opening bid with the following hand?

♠ none
♡ K 10 6 5 4 2
◇ A 10 8 7 6 2
♣ 7

Like mine, I suppose, rather mixed. It is the type of hand that can make a great many tricks if partner has a fit in one of your suits; but there can be disaster in store if there is no good fit—your partner is unlikely to place you with only seven high card points. Still, it can't be denied that the best way to find out if a fit exists is to start bidding at the earliest opportunity. This was a hand from the 1957 trials:

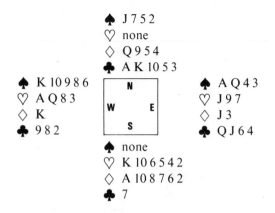

♠ J 7 5 2
♡ none
♢ Q 9 5 4
♣ A K 10 5 3

♠ K 10 9 8 6   ♠ A Q 4 3
♡ A Q 8 3   ♡ J 9 7
♢ K   ♢ J 3
♣ 9 8 2   ♣ Q J 6 4

♠ none
♡ K 10 6 5 4 2
♢ A 10 8 7 6 2
♣ 7

My team-mates duly bid and made Five Diamonds with the North–
South cards—a sound enough contract. However, at the other
table South, the late Albert Rose, rated his hand more highly
and this was the bidding:

South (Rose)	West	North (Gardener)	East
1 ♡	1 ♠	2 ♣	2 ♠
3 ♢	pass	5 ♢	pass
6 ♢	pass	pass	pass

Against Six Diamonds I led a Spade after which correct timing
by declarer should yield twelve tricks. The point of the hand is
that South must ruff dummy's fourth Spade before he attempts
to ruff the fourth round of Hearts with the Queen of Diamonds.
South can start by cashing the Ace and King of Clubs and ruffing
another Spade. The next five tricks are made by cross-ruffing
Hearts and Spades, then declarer can ruff a Club with the ten of
Diamonds and lead a Heart to score a trick with the Queen of
Diamonds.

However, the play did not go quite that way. South erred by
ruffing a Club in hand too early, with the result that when he
trumped a Heart with the Queen of Diamonds East was able to
discard a Spade to leave the position shown on the next page.

As you can see, when the Jack of Spades is led from dummy, East
can defeat the contract by ruffing with the Jack of Diamonds.
But South's light opening bid finally paid off when East decided

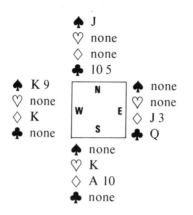

```
              ♠ J
              ♡ none
              ◇ none
              ♣ 10 5
♠ K 9        ┌─────────┐     ♠ none
♡ none       │    N    │     ♡ none
◇ K          │ W     E │     ◇ J 3
♣ none       │    S    │     ♣ Q
             └─────────┘
              ♠ none
              ♡ K
              ◇ A 10
              ♣ none
```

that South must have both the Ace and the King of Diamonds
left and that to trump with the Jack of Diamonds would merely
concede an overtrick. The match was close and the 1 international
match point that this would cost might be vital. So East discarded
a Club and it was all over.

When the above hand originally appeared, I see that I took a
safety-play. To prevent a deluge of correspondence I hastened to add
that, yes, I could have defeated the slam by leading the King of Diamonds at trick 1. It was a safety-play that worked—I received no
letters!

The next hand, from the closing stages of the 1969 Gold Cup, was
a good one for the technician. Unfortunately, declarer missed a
pointer and did not give himself every available chance.

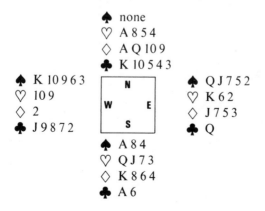

```
                  ♠ none
                  ♡ A 8 5 4
                  ◇ A Q 10 9
                  ♣ K 10 5 4 3
♠ K 10 9 6 3     ┌─────────┐     ♠ Q J 7 5 2
♡ 10 9           │    N    │     ♡ K 6 2
◇ 2              │ W     E │     ◇ J 7 5 3
♣ J 9 8 7 2      │    S    │     ♣ Q
                 └─────────┘
                  ♠ A 8 4
                  ♡ Q J 7 3
                  ◇ K 8 6 4
                  ♣ A 6
```

North dealt at game-all and South ended in Six Hearts against which West led the ten of Spades. Declarer made a good start to a difficult hand when he ruffed low in dummy and continued with a low Heart. East went in with the King and returned a low Heart to dummy's Ace. South came to hand with the Ace of Clubs and ruffed his other losing Spade, then came back with the King of Diamonds to draw the last trump. Although a finesse of the ten of Clubs wins at this point, not unnaturally declarer preferred to play a Club to the King to give himself the chance of a 3–3 break in the suit. However, when East showed out and the Diamonds proved to be 4–1 there were only eleven tricks.

South missed an inference in the play. When East went in with the King of Hearts and returned a Heart it was safe to assume that he had not started with four trumps (when he would surely have played low). Instead of winning with the Ace of Hearts in dummy, declarer can win in hand with the Jack and ruff his Spade with the Ace of Hearts, then come back with the Ace of Clubs to draw the last trump. The vital difference is that South still has the King of Diamonds in hand and when West proves to have started with five Clubs it is easy to cater for East holding length in Diamonds by playing the Ace and the Queen.

It is quite a well-known stratagem, if you are void in a suit, to under-lead several top honours in another suit in the hope of giving partner the lead and so gaining a ruff. Rather more of a rarity

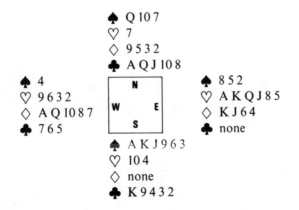

is a hand where both pairs of the same team attempt a similar play. When the time came for comparing scores on this hand, from an early round of the 1964 Gold Cup, it became clear that they had met with mixed success.

East dealt at love-all and the bidding at one table went:

South	West	North	East
			1 ♡
2 ♠	3 ♡	4 ♠	6 ♡
dble	pass	pass	pass

It was not a scientific auction and no one could have had much idea as to whether the final contract was reasonable or not. However, South, in an attempt to justify his double, hit on the spectacular lead of the nine of Spades. North dutifully won with the Queen and was not hard put to it to deduce that a Diamond return was required. South ruffed and the contract failed by one trick. It was still uncertain whether this would be a good result, for Six Spades by South was on unless there was a Club lead.

At the other table the players got their money's worth in the bidding:

South	West	North	East
			1 ♡
1 ♠	2 ♡	3 ♠	4 ♡
4 ♠	5 ◇	pass	pass
5 ♠	pass	pass	6 ♣!
dble	6 ♡	pass	pass
6 ♠	pass	pass	dble
pass	pass	pass	

The revealing bid, of course, was East's Six Clubs. It was clear to West that this was a lead-directing effort and he led the five of Clubs to give East an immediate ruff. In East's position you or I might simply cash the Ace of Hearts to ensure defeat of the slam, but East determined to try for the maximum penalty. He returned the two of Hearts, hoping that West could win and lead another Club. Unfortunately South (who had seen this sort of position before) went in with the ten of Hearts. When this held he was able to claim.

On balance, the under-leaders scored 100 points in one room but lost 1210 in the other!

If you are familiar with the international match point scale you will appreciate that the largest possible score on a hand from match-play is 25 i.m.p.—scored for a difference of 3500 or more aggregate points. Why, then, did the Swiss team claim to have scored a world record when they lost 35 i.m.p. in their match against Egypt at Torquay in 1961? This is what happened:

```
                    ♠ K Q J 10 7
                    ♡ 10 9 8 6 4
                    ◊ none
                    ♣ A Q 5
  ♠ A 3 2                           ♠ 5 4
  ♡ K 2             N               ♡ A Q J 5
  ◊ A K 9 5 4 3   W   E             ◊ J 10 7 6 2
  ♣ 10 2            S               ♣ J 6
                    ♠ 9 8 6
                    ♡ 7 3
                    ◊ Q 8
                    ♣ K 9 8 7 4 3
```

South dealt at game-all and, with Switzerland North–South, West opened One Diamond. This is how the bidding was recorded:

South	West	North	East
pass	1 ◊	1 ♠	3 ◊
2 ♠	2 NT	4 ♠	pass
pass	pass		

No, there is no misprint, it was a mis-heard bid; and clearly West did not appreciate that anything odd had happened. According to the rules, his bid of Two No Trumps condoned the previous insufficient call. There was no problem in the play and declarer scored 620 points. At the other table East–West played in Five Diamonds to collect a further 600 points—apparently a gain to Switzerland of 17 match points. However, all was not well, and there was more to the confusion at the first table than appeared on the official score sheet. So much so that, before the second half of the match was played, the Tournament Committee ruled

148

that the board should be replayed. This was its second appearance:

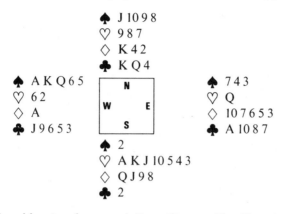

```
                    ♠ J 10 9 8
                    ♡ 9 8 7
                    ◊ K 4 2
                    ♣ K Q 4
    ♠ A K Q 6 5          N          ♠ 7 4 3
    ♡ 6 2          W         E      ♡ Q
    ◊ A                              ◊ 10 7 6 5 3
    ♣ J 9 6 5 3         S           ♣ A 10 8 7
                    ♠ 2
                    ♡ A K J 10 5 4 3
                    ◊ Q J 9 8
                    ♣ 2
```

At both tables South opened Four Hearts. The Egyptian West over-called with Four Spades and duly made ten tricks, but the Swiss West elected to double. He started with the Ace of Spades and the Ace of Diamonds, then switched to a Club. A Diamond return would at least have defeated the contract, but East found the position difficult to read and returned a Spade. That was another game to Egypt, and a total gain of 18 match points. You can see the substance of the Swiss claim now—they had a gain of 17 taken away from them and a loss of 18 substituted, a net loss of 35 international match points on the board!

A correspondent once wrote that he "supposed that in top-class match-play the bidding and play were identical at most tables". Well, quite apart from the variety of bidding systems currently in use, you have only to look at the widely divergent answers given by the panellists of the bidding competitions in bridge magazines to see that the opinions of practitioners reputedly playing the same system are not always the same.

Take this problem. At game-all South holds:

```
    ♠ A 4 3
    ♡ 10 7 5
    ◊ 10 8 6 4 2
    ♣ 10 5
```

South	West	North	East
	1 ♠	2 ♠	pass
3 ◇	pass	4 ♣	pass
?			

Between them, the panel argued variously but lucidly in favour of
Four No Trumps, Five Clubs, Four Diamonds, Four Hearts and
Four Spades!

Or consider this deal from the 1957 International Trials, played
at six tables:

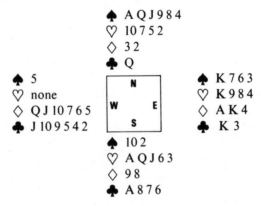

```
              ♠ A Q J 9 8 4
              ♡ 10 7 5 2
              ◇ 3 2
              ♣ Q
♠ 5                              ♠ K 7 6 3
♡ none          N                ♡ K 9 8 4
◇ Q J 10 7 6 5  W      E          ◇ A K 4
♣ J 10 9 5 4 2     S              ♣ K 3
              ♠ 10 2
              ♡ A Q J 6 3
              ◇ 9 8
              ♣ A 8 7 6
```

West dealt at love-all. At the first table West passed and North
opened Three Spades where he was allowed to play. He could
have made his contract but went astray at the end to go one
down. At the next table, without opposition bidding, East–West
reached Four Diamonds and made twelve tricks when declarer
threw all of dummy's Spades away on his Clubs. Two West
players opened Three Diamonds and ended in Five Diamonds,
but only one made his contract. His counterpart played on Clubs
before drawing trumps and so sustained a ruff. One North judged
his hand to be worth a one-bid and after a fiercely contested
auction South played in Four Hearts and failed, after complicated
play, by one trick.

At the last table, where I was involved, North opened Three
Spades. After two passes West re-opened with an unusual Three
No Trumps—clearly for the minors. Sitting East, I gauged that
my cards in the major suits would be sufficient and passed. Against

Three No Trumps North led the Queen of Spades and was allowed to hold the trick. The ten of Hearts would have been a good card to play now, but North switched to the Queen of Clubs and this was covered by the King and Ace. There was still time for South to play back a Spade to North's Ace, but he returned a Club and West had the remaining tricks.

Some players, especially the rubber-bridge kind, are always complaining that they never get dealt their fair share of aces and kings. They would have had little cause for complaint if they had picked up the South hand on this deal, taken from the American trials of 1967:

```
                    ♠ J 2
                    ♡ J 8 5 3
                    ◇ Q 8 7 4
                    ♣ 9 5 2
    ♠ K 8 5 3      ┌─────────┐      ♠ 10 9 6 4
    ♡ 10 7 4       │    N    │      ♡ Q 9 2
    ◇ J 9 2        │ W     E │      ◇ 10 6 5 3
    ♣ 8 7 6        │    S    │      ♣ 4 3
                   └─────────┘
                    ♠ A Q 7
                    ♡ A K 6
                    ◇ A K
                    ♣ A K Q J 10
```

South dealt at game-all but in spite of his wealth of high cards the hand was not easy for him to bid. After he had started with Two Clubs and heard the not unexpected reply of Two Diamonds, the textbooks suggest Four No Trumps, implying a balanced hand with about 29 points. This might be right with a 4–3–3–3 distribution, but it did not work well on this hand. Several pairs started this way, some advancing to Six No Trumps and some stopping safely in Four No Trumps. One South, equipped with elaborate asking bids, discovered that his partner held no kings and one queen—the Queen of Diamonds. Not unreasonably, he stopped in Three No Trumps.

Eleven tricks were the limit in No Trumps against careful defence, as some discovered to their cost. After a passive Club lead South wins and unblocks the Ace and King of Diamonds. If

151

he leads the Queen of Spades next West must duck, but if South tries a low Spade West must rush in with his king. So declarer is denied access to dummy's Queen of Diamonds.

Only one pair reached the best contract. After 2 C–2 D, South first showed his suit by bidding Three Clubs. North gave a second negative response and now South jumped to Five No Trumps. With a queen, two jacks, three trumps and a possible ruffing value it was not difficult for North to advance to Six Clubs.

Against Six Clubs West led a trump. Declarer won and led the Queen of Spades to West's King. On a trump continuation he planned to draw trumps, cash the Ace and King of Diamonds and cross to the Jack of Spades for a Heart discard on the Queen of Diamonds. However, West played back a Spade to remove dummy's Jack. Now South drew one more round of trumps, re- leased his top Diamonds and, with a flourish, ruffed the Ace of Spades on the table to get at his twelfth trick.

Strong two-suited hands are always difficult to develop when the opponents open the bidding against you, and this hand from the 1959 Gold Cup final was no exception.

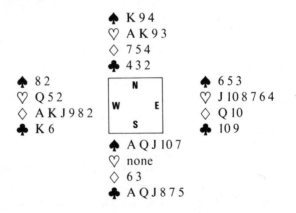

West dealt at game-all and at one table elected to open with an off-beat One No Trump East bid Two Hearts and South Three Hearts. After a pass by West, North tried Three No Trumps and South made a good decision when he bid Four Spades rather than show his Clubs. North had a good hand, but it looked as though a lot of his values in Hearts would be wasted. Furthermore, a bid in the opponent's suit in the protective position does not suggest quite as strong a hand as if the over-call were direct, so North decided to pass. It was a wise decision, for Four Spades was the only game that could be made.

At the other table West preferred to open One Diamond and the bidding went as follows (it is easy to smile, but both players had problems!):

South	West	North	East
	1 ◇	pass	pass
2 ◇	pass	2 ♡	pass
3 ♣	pass	3 ♠	pass
4 ♠	pass	5 ♣	pass
5 ♠	pass	6 ♣	pass
pass	pass		

If South's Two Diamonds was the best re-opening bid, North's Two Hearts and South's Three Clubs were correct. But what of North's Three Spades? Presumably he argued that as partner did not seem to approve of Hearts he must have a black two-suiter, and merely wanted to hear which suit North preferred. In that case perhaps North should just pass Four Spades. However, he chose to go back to Five Clubs and South took this as showing a Club feature with the Spade suit agreed as trumps. Lacking any control in Diamonds he signed off in Five Spades only to be returned to Clubs again. It was not difficult for the defence to take two Diamond tricks and wait for a trump trick to come.

Look at the North–South hands overleaf: it is not difficult to see that Six Clubs is an excellent contract—all that need be done is to ruff a Spade in the short trump hand and there are twelve tricks. However, at none of the six tables in play in the 1960 trials was Six Clubs reached.

At all tables South chose to open Two No Trumps and most Norths preferred to start their investigations with a Stayman Three Clubs. It became clear that there were limitations in this method when it came to finding a 5–3 minor suit fit! One North–South pair ended in Clubs, but as they had adventured their way

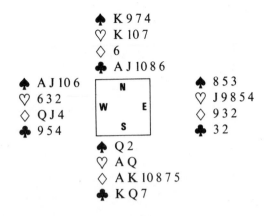

                    ♠ K 9 7 4
                    ♡ K 10 7
                    ◇ 6
                    ♣ A J 10 8 6

♠ A J 10 6   ♠ 8 5 3
♡ 6 3 2   N   ♡ J 9 8 5 4
◇ Q J 4   W   E   ◇ 9 3 2
♣ 9 5 4   S   ♣ 3 2

                    ♠ Q 2
                    ♡ A Q
                    ◇ A K 10 8 7 5
                    ♣ K Q 7

to the seven-level and were unlucky enough to attract a Spade
lead from East they did not score well. (On any other lead Seven
Clubs makes, for there is time to establish the long Diamonds.)

The rest of the field preferred to take their chances in Six No
Trumps. One declarer, faced with a passive Club lead, tried an
interesting line of play. He won on the table and immediately
ducked a Diamond to West. If West did not hold the Ace of
Spades and failed to find a Spade switch there would be enough
tricks on an even Diamond break. However, West had no difficulty with his lead at trick 3.

The other declarers in Six No Trumps decided to lead the Queen
of Spades at trick 2, establishing their eleventh trick and correct-
ing the timing for a possible squeeze. West took his Ace and
played back the Jack of Spades to the King. Now the play was
straightforward: South played off the Ace of Hearts and followed
with the rest of his clubs and the King of Hearts. At the end West
was hopelessly squeezed with the ten of Spades and the Q J 4 of
Diamonds.

In effect West's defence relied on finding his partner with the
protected ten of Diamonds, for then there would be no squeeze.
It is not immediately obvious, but a return of the Queen (or Jack)
of Diamonds from West when he is in with the Ace of Spades
breaks up the squeeze. Try it and see. South cannot cash five Clubs
and three Hearts and still end with the lead in his own hand. It
would have been a thoughtful defence to find, but in the event
none of the West players rose to the occasion.

Signalling is one of the defenders' most valuable weapons—if properly used—and yet not all players use it to the best advantage. Some actively discourage their partners from signalling ("Don't throw high cards at me. *I* know what to play!), some choose a sensible compromise by signalling when they think that it will help their partner more than declarer, and some make their high-lows with remorseless regularity. It is always a pleasure to play against a pair who signal their suit lengths automatically—suppose you have started with A K x facing Q x x x. If the Ace and King find both opponents following normally without signalling, you can virtually rely on a 3–3 break and do not have to test the possibility immediately.

A classic case of a signal assisting the declarer came up in a European Championship some years ago.

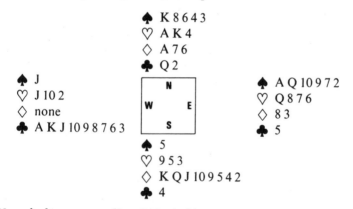

```
                    ♠ K 8 6 4 3
                    ♡ A K 4
                    ◇ A 7 6
                    ♣ Q 2
  ♠ J                                   ♠ A Q 10 9 7 2
  ♡ J 10 2              N               ♡ Q 8 7 6
  ◇ none          W         E           ◇ 8 3
  ♣ A K J 10 9 8 7 6 3     S            ♣ 5
                    ♠ 5
                    ♡ 9 5 3
                    ◇ K Q J 10 9 5 4 2
                    ♣ 4
```

West dealt at game-all and the bidding was short and sweet:

South	West	North	East
	5 ♣	dble	pass
5 ◇	pass	pass	pass

West led a top Club and South ruffed the second round. However, before he did so, East had to make a discard and unwisely selected the ten of Spades to indicate his firm hold in the suit. His grip may have been firm enough when play started but he soon found that it had been fatally weakened by his discard.

South drew one round of trumps with the King of Diamonds, then followed with the five of Spades to the Jack, King and Ace.

155

East returned a trump to dummy's Ace and declarer continued with the eight of Spades from the table. East covered with the nine and South ruffed. Next came a trump to the seven, and the six of Spades followed. Gloomily East covered with the Queen but the position had become all too clear. There were still two Heart entries to the table and declarer was able to take a ruffing finesse with the remaining four and three of Spades through East's seven and two. The losing Heart went away and declarer had eleven tricks. It is curious to note that the only Spade East can afford to throw (if he must discard one at all) is the two!

11
Nerves and High-level Contracts

Do you reckon that you have strong nerves at bridge? Especially where high level, doubled and vulnerable contracts are concerned? I like the story of one of our international players, facing the mercurial John Collings as partner for the first time. John had gone into a long explanation, before play started, as to what a particular type of jump over-call showed. Our hero, hoping that the situation did not arise, placidly agreed to include John's latest brain-child in their repertoire. Needless to say, on the first board they played, he found that he had to introducè a suit of 5 4 3 2 (or four to the five, as they say) at the five-level, vulnerable against not vulnerable, with, as he put it, only a two-to-one-on chance of it being one of his partner's suits. Because, needless to say, he had already forgotten just which two suits partner was supposed to be showing. There was a happy ending; he bid Five Hearts (which the partnership couldn't make) but the opposition decided to sacrifice.

How would you have coped with a dilemma that faced Tony Milford in a Camrose Cup match between England and Wales? The dealer on your right opens One No Trump, not vulnerable, and you pass, holding:

♠ 7 6 2
♡ K 10 8 4
◇ Q 5
♣ K 7 6 3

Three No Trumps on your left, double from your partner! You begin to think about your lead. Partner can hardly have doubled on general values, so presumably he has a strong suit. You decide that you are going to lead a Spade, but after two passes the player on your left takes out into Four Diamonds. North and East pass and it is up to you after this bidding:

South	West	North	East
			1 NT
pass	3 NT	dble	pass
pass	4 ◊	pass	pass

Now it is clear that West's raise to Three No Trumps was based on long Diamonds. Can you let them play in Four Diamonds, undoubled, or rely on partner's double and bid Four Spades?

Oh, I forgot to mention that you were vulnerable and playing on *Bridgerama*! Fairly confident that he had the situation weighed up, Milford bid Four Spades on the 7 6 2. When this was promptly doubled by West he felt less confident, but there was nowhere to go, so he passed. This was the full hand:

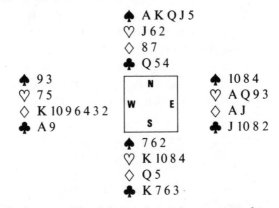

West led the Ace of Clubs and South was one down in Four Spades doubled. It was a fair result because Three No Trumps is on unless a Spade is led. At the other table the English pair made a part-score in Diamonds.

My opponents at rubber bridge recently showed less good nerves when they held as East–West:

West	East
x x	A K Q J x x x
J x x x	x x
x x x	x x x
J x x x	x

158

East, not vulnerable, passed in the hope of bringing off a coup. I opened One No Trump as South, my partner gave me Three No Trumps, and East now doubled. West, recalling that his partner had passed originally, took out into Four Clubs, so we collected 500 (less honours) against Four Spades instead of losing 800 in Three No Trumps.

Are you sometimes at a loss for words when your partner has committed an atrocity? I can generally find words, but they are not always the right ones. I have made a resolution to be guided by a new formula, established during a preliminary stage of the French trials of 1969. This was the deal that provided the occasion:

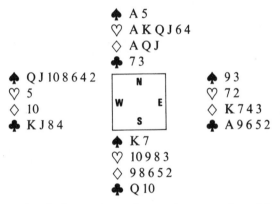

```
              ♠ A 5
              ♡ A K Q J 6 4
              ◇ A Q J
              ♣ 7 3

♠ Q J 10 8 6 4 2    N       ♠ 9 3
♡ 5                         ♡ 7 2
◇ 10          W       E     ◇ K 7 4 3
♣ K J 8 4           S       ♣ A 9 6 5 2

              ♠ K 7
              ♡ 10 9 8 3
              ◇ 9 8 6 5 2
              ♣ Q 10
```

North was the dealer and North–South were vulnerable. Playing for a vulnerable game, the North–South players were sometimes pushed overboard. At one table the bidding went:

South	West	North	East
		1 ♣	pass
1 ◇	1 NT	4 ♡	pass
pass	4 ♠	pass	pass
5 ♡	pass	pass	pass

Here North–South were playing the Blue Club. South had a maximum for his negative response of One Diamond and was not wrong to try Five Hearts. In my opinion, North, with several losers, should have doubled Four Spades instead of making a forcing pass.

159

The best result for North–South occurred when the winners of the trial, Chemla–Lebel, were opposed to Ficot and Gubert. North opened Two Clubs and the bidding continued:

South	West	North	East
		2 ♣	pass
2 ◇	3 ♠	pass	pass
4 ♡	pass	5 ♡	pass
6 ♡	pass	pass	pass

Here, too, North's forcing pass over Three Spades was pointless: he should have bid a straightforward Four Hearts. And of course his raise to Five Hearts was open to question.

However, West led the ten of Diamonds and East, in with the King, returned a Spade at trick 2, presenting the declarer with twelve tricks. What East was thinking about is difficult to imagine. West then made his memorable speech:

Tu es mon meilleur ami. C'est la seule raison pour laquelle j'accepte de m'asseoir à une table de bridge en face de toi. Je supporte beaucoup de choses . . . mais ça vraiment, pour les nerfs, c'est trop.

(You are my best friend. That is the sole reason why I agree to sit opposite you at the bridge table. I endure many things . . . but this, for the nerves, is really too much.)

"Tu es mon meilleur ami . . ." I'll remember that!

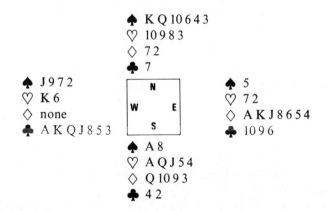

        ♠ K Q 10 6 4 3
        ♡ 10 9 8 3
        ◇ 7 2
        ♣ 7

♠ J 9 7 2   ♠ 5
♡ K 6   ♡ 7 2
◇ none   ◇ A K J 8 6 5 4
♣ A K Q J 8 5 3   ♣ 10 9 6

        ♠ A 8
        ♡ A Q J 5 4
        ◇ Q 10 9 3
        ♣ 4 2

They say nothing is certain except death and taxes, but the aspiring bridge player may add to the list of certainties that every player is dealt thirteen cards. Much good play, offensive or defensive, rests on this simple but often neglected foundation. You may think declarer was blessed with strong nerves or a long neck on the following deal, but try counting up to thirteen. . . .

West was the dealer with East–West game and this was the bidding in a team game:

South	West	North	East
	1 ♣	1 ♠	2 ◇
2 ♡	3 ♣	3 ♡	4 ♣
4 ♡	5 ♣	pass	pass
dble	pass	5 ♡	dble
pass	pass	pass	

West led the King of Clubs and continued with the Ace. Declarer ruffed in dummy and lost a Heart finesse to the King. West returned a Heart and South won in his own hand. Declarer now played Ace and another Spade, finessing the ten. When the finesse held he discarded all his Diamonds on the Spades and made Five Hearts doubled. If he had not finessed the ten of Spades he would have gone down: he can set up the Spades and get back with a trump, but he can dispose of only three Diamonds.

It was an annoying hand for the defenders, who had four top tricks but couldn't get to them after the opening lead. "With a void in Diamonds you might have tried underleading your Clubs," East remarked; somewhat unreasonably, for it did not look to West as though desperation measures were needed.

The interesting point is, why did South finesse the ten of Spades on the second round? A premonition and strong nerves? It was not so difficult, really, if you remember the bidding. West was known to hold two Hearts, and the Club distribution, in view of East's raise, was likely to be 7–3. As for Diamonds, West had had two opportunities to lead the suit bid by his partner and had spurned both. He must be void and that placed him with 4–2–0–7 distribution.

Now for a chance to relax your nerves. Has it ever occurred to you that it is sometimes easier to play in a contract of seven than six? That was certainly the case on this deal from the semi-final match in the Olympiad between the USA (who lost to Italy in the final) and the Netherlands in 1968.

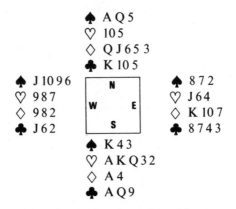

```
                    ♠ A Q 5
                    ♡ 10 5
                    ◊ Q J 6 5 3
                    ♣ K 10 5
    ♠ J 10 9 6     ┌─────────┐    ♠ 8 7 2
    ♡ 9 8 7        │    N    │    ♡ J 6 4
    ◊ 9 8 2        │ W     E │    ◊ K 10 7
    ♣ J 6 2        │    S    │    ♣ 8 7 4 3
                   └─────────┘
                    ♠ K 4 3
                    ♡ A K Q 3 2
                    ◊ A 4
                    ♣ A Q 9
```

North dealt and North–South were vulnerable. Despite the score, the Dutch North opened One Diamond. South responded One Heart and North rebid One No Trump, which South raised to Seven No Trumps. A Club was led and the play took no time at all. Needing the Diamond finesse and a 3–3 break in Hearts, North quickly wrapped up the 18 per cent grand slam.

The American bidding was more orthodox:

South (Kay)	North (Kaplan)
	pass
2 ♣	3 ◊
3 NT	4 ♠
6 NT	pass

How should South handle the play after the lead of the Jack of Spades? "The majority of the audience," reports the bulletin issued at the tournament, "favoured winning in hand and leading a low diamond. So they were rather hurt when, after a ten-minute huddle, declarer decided to test the hearts first."

I have given it a twenty-minute huddle and I cannot see what prompted Norman Kay to tackle Hearts before Diamonds. If the Hearts are 3–3 he always has twelve tricks. If they are 4–2 he will have to take the Diamond finesse later and will have given up all squeeze chances. There is nothing to choose between taking an orthodox finesse of the Queen of Diamonds or leading a low Diamond from hand. Suppose you win the opening lead in dummy and run the Queen of Diamonds. If it holds, you can afford the safety play in Hearts, leading low from hand towards the 10 5, as a precaution against J x x x x on your left. If the Diamond finesse loses you have eleven tricks on top and will win if the Diamonds are 3–3 or the Hearts 3–3; you can also squeeze either opponent who may hold the long Diamonds and the long Hearts.

As I said, it was much easier to play in seven!

Again at a very high level, the next hand exhibits a tactical manœuvre that tends to be underestimated and has a human as well as a psychological point.

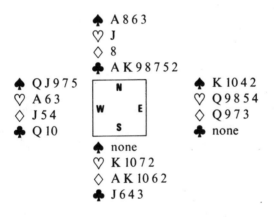

                ♠ A 8 6 3
                ♡ J
                ◇ 8
                ♣ A K 9 8 7 5 2

♠ Q J 9 7 5   ♠ K 10 4 2
♡ A 6 3   N   ♡ Q 9 8 5 4
◇ J 5 4   W   E   ◇ Q 9 7 3
♣ Q 10   S   ♣ none

                ♠ none
                ♡ K 10 7 2
                ◇ A K 10 6 2
                ♣ J 6 4 3

The deal came up in the World Pairs Olympiad of 1966 and it so happened that in an early round American pairs were in opposition at two tables. East dealt at game-all and there was a remarkable similarity in the two auctions:

South	West	North	East
(Fisher)	(Stayman)	(J. Jacoby)	(Kaplan)
1 ♦	1 ♠	2 ♣	3 ♠
4 ♣	pass	4 NT	pass
6 ♣	pass	7 ♣	pass
pass	pass		

South	West	North	East
(Robinson)	(Rapee)	(Jordan)	(Koytchou)
1 ♦	1 ♠	2 ♣	4 ♠
5 ♣	pass	5 ♠	dble
pass	pass	7 ♣	pass
pass	pass		

A Spade was led at both tables and the declarer landed the grand slam by discarding a Heart on a Diamond and taking three Spade ruffs in the South hand.

If you are thinking "What sort of experts are these, to bid a grand slam missing an Ace?" forget it. They both knew.

And if you are thinking, "Well, perhaps they wanted to give a leg-up to their friends," forget that too. Bridge players are not like that.

On the contrary, it is clear that both North players were entranced by the possibility of bringing off a coup against players from their own circle. They worked it out like this: "We are probably missing one of the red aces, but East, who is on lead, won't have that ace. If he suspects a trap at all he will lead a Spade, thinking that we do not expect such an obvious lead. Alternatively, he may lead a passive trump. And even if he does lead a red suit he may choose the wrong one."

Let me add hastily that I wouldn't recommend such a daring coup at rubber bridge. But in a pairs event it is a fair gamble, so long as you can be sure that the opening leader does not hold the missing ace.

The trump coup is generally thought of as a risky form of play suitable for experts only, but it is one of the easier types of endgame to plan and execute. Here is an example from rubber bridge where I had to sit and watch my partner lose a grand slam. This was not good for my nerves!

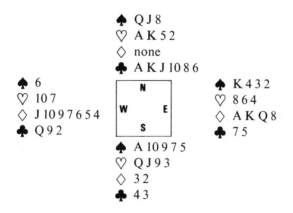

```
                    ♠ Q J 8
                    ♡ A K 5 2
                    ◇ none
                    ♣ A K J 10 8 6
    ♠ 6                              ♠ K 4 3 2
    ♡ 10 7          ┌─────────┐      ♡ 8 6 4
    ◇ J 10 9 7 6 5 4│    N    │      ◇ A K Q 8
    ♣ Q 9 2         │ W     E │      ♣ 7 5
                    │    S    │
                    └─────────┘
                    ♠ A 10 9 7 5
                    ♡ Q J 9 3
                    ◇ 3 2
                    ♣ 4 3
```

Our opponents put up a psychic barrage, and as sometimes happens this had the effect of propelling our side to a higher level than we might have reached otherwise. With East the dealer at love-all the bidding went:

South	West	North	East
			1 ◇
1 ♠	2 NT	3 ◇	pass
3 ♠	5 ◇	6 ♠	7 ◇
pass	pass	7 ♠	pass
pass	pass		

Having a rather poor hand, my partner probably ought to have doubled the Seven Diamonds sacrifice. When he omitted to do so I assumed that there must be a good play for Seven Spades.

The Diamond lead was ruffed in dummy and West showed out on the second round of trumps. It was obvious now that South would need a trump coup, and the first essential was to reduce his trumps to the same length as East's. He accomplished this successfully by ruffing the third round of Clubs, East discarding a Heart meanwhile. A Heart was led to the Ace and declarer then begin to lead out the winning Clubs. East hastily discarded his third Heart and this was the position at trick 9:

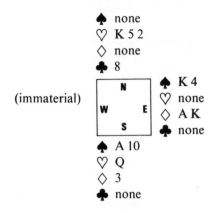

```
              ♠ none
              ♡ K 5 2
              ◇ none
              ♣ 8
                          ♠ K 4
(immaterial)      N       ♡ none
              W       E   ◇ A K
                  S       ♣ none
              ♠ A 10
              ♡ Q
              ◇ 3
              ♣ none
```

East discarded a Diamond on the last Club and South was doomed whether he let go a Heart or a Diamond. He threw the Heart. East ruffed the next lead and South had to lose a Diamond at the finish.

The declarer's mistake was in failing to cash a second Heart before playing off the good Clubs. He has three Club winners in dummy and must keep the same number of side-suit cards in his own hand. If the Heart is ruffed by East, that's too bad.

Do you want to be in a grand slam that depends on a finesse? Mathematically speaking, no, but so often when there are twelve sure tricks there are extra chances of squeezing out the thirteenth without recourse to the finesse. This hand from the Lederer Memorial Trophy of 1972 is a case in point:

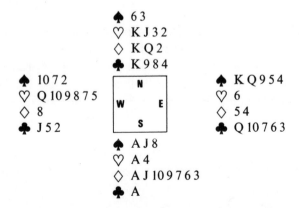

```
                  ♠ 6 3
                  ♡ K J 3 2
                  ◇ K Q 2
                  ♣ K 9 8 4
    ♠ 10 7 2          N        ♠ K Q 9 5 4
    ♡ Q 10 9 8 7 5             ♡ 6
    ◇ 8          W       E     ◇ 5 4
    ♣ J 5 2          S         ♣ Q 10 7 6 3
                  ♠ A J 8
                  ♡ A 4
                  ◇ A J 10 9 7 6 3
                  ♣ A
```

North dealt at game-all and passed. At most tables South was content with a small slam in Diamonds, but at one table he pushed on to Seven Diamonds.

West led the ten of Hearts—in itself a risky lead against a grand slam. If South had held the Jack of Hearts instead of North the lead would have conceded declarer's thirteenth trick immediately. However, the lead served its purpose, for South was convinced that the Heart finesse would be wrong. Hoping that East had started with Q x or Q x x in Hearts, he played low from dummy and won in hand. Two rounds of trumps were followed by a low Heart to the King to reveal the bad news.

It looked as though South had ruined his chances, but declarer was not a player to give up easily. He played off the Ace of Clubs and followed with his remaining trumps, keeping K 9 8 of Clubs in dummy. As far as West was concerned, this was not a problem hand. For his last three cards he kept the ten of Spades, the Queen of Hearts and the Jack of Clubs. East, however, had to make his final discard from K Q of Spades and Q 10 of Clubs. Yes, you've guessed. Unsure of the whereabouts of the Jack of Clubs (which West should have thrown at the first opportunity), he let go the Queen of Spades, hoping that his partner was still able to guard the Spades. Now South made the last three tricks with A J 8 of Spades.

Under what circumstances should you and your partner bid a grand slam? Odds of 2–1 on are widely quoted and look correct mathematically, for, if vulnerable, you score an extra 750 points for bidding and making seven, but stand to lose 100+1430 points (the penalty, together with what you would have collected if you had stopped in six). However, the odds can be affected in two ways. Consider these hands:

West	East
A J 10 8 6	K 9 7 4
A 5	8 6
K Q 3 2	A J 10 8 6
A 8	K 4

Suppose West plays in Six Spades on a Heart lead. Apart from the possibility of a 4–0 Diamond break, the contract will be made if declarer can pick up the Queen of trumps successfully—a reasonable gamble. But if he *can* locate the Queen of Spades, he will make all thirteen tricks. In other words, he will be better placed to have bid seven rather than six—the chances of success are equal and the rewards for seven are greater.

The other situation in which it pays to go on to a grand slam is one where the opponents have found a cheap sacrifice against your small slam. Then, even a relatively small chance of gaining the grand slam bonus may give a higher expectation of gain than a small, safe penalty. This hand came up in the 1967 Crockfords Cup final:

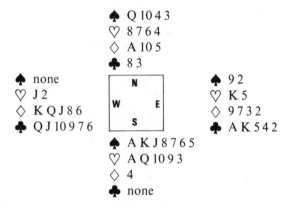

```
                    ♠ Q 10 4 3
                    ♡ 8 7 6 4
                    ◇ A 10 5
                    ♣ 8 3
  ♠ none          ┌─────────┐      ♠ 9 2
  ♡ J 2          │    N    │      ♡ K 5
  ◇ K Q J 8 6    │ W     E │      ◇ 9 7 3 2
  ♣ Q J 10 9 7 6 │    S    │      ♣ A K 5 4 2
                  └─────────┘
                    ♠ A K J 8 7 6 5
                    ♡ A Q 10 9 3
                    ◇ 4
                    ♣ none
```

South dealt with North–South vulnerable and this was the bidding:

South	West	North	East
2 ♠	2 NT (*a*)	3 ◇ (*b*)	6 ♣
6 ♠	pass	pass	7 ♣
7 ♠	pass	pass	pass

(*a*) Unusual, suggesting length in the minor suits. (*b*) As Diamonds was one of the suits in which West had implied length, South correctly interpreted the bid of Three Diamonds as agreeing Spades and showing control in Diamonds.

After ruffing the Club lead and drawing trumps, South correctly finessed the Queen of Hearts—a play that won as the cards lay and would also have won if West had held the Jack of Hearts alone.

Would South have got it right, I wonder, if West had made the inspired choice of the two of Hearts for his opening lead? There would now be a tremendous temptation to play East for both missing honours.

12
Squeezes and their Defence

How would you fancy your chances of making Five Clubs on the deal below? West begins with two top Diamonds and switches to a trump:

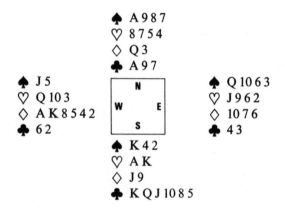

	♠ A 9 8 7	
	♡ 8 7 5 4	
	◇ Q 3	
	♣ A 9 7	
♠ J 5		♠ Q 10 6 3
♡ Q 10 3		♡ J 9 6 2
◇ A K 8 5 4 2		◇ 10 7 6
♣ 6 2		♣ 4 3
	♠ K 4 2	
	♡ A K	
	◇ J 9	
	♣ K Q J 10 8 5	

Prospects may not seem good, as you appear to have a certain loser in Spades. You manage it by squeezing. Bridge writers often make squeeze play sound more difficult than it is, hedging it around with important-sounding formulas. I recommend the direct route: just ask yourself if there is a chance of finding the same opponent with control of two suits. On this occasion you need to find the same opponent in charge of Spades and Hearts.

You draw trumps, cash two top Hearts, cross to dummy with a Club and ruff the third round of Hearts. That is essential; it creates the situation where only one opponent can control the Heart suit. You lead out all but one trump, arriving at the position at the top of the next page. On the last Club you discard a Spade from dummy and East can go home.

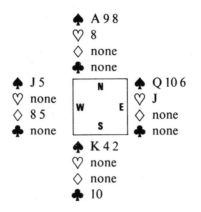

Perhaps you have noted that West could break up the entries for this squeeze by leading a Spade at trick 3? If your opponents are that good, the best advice I can give you is to cut into another game!

Of course, squeeze play has its traps. For example, how did Roger Trezel, the French star, fail to make Six Hearts on the deal below after West had led the Ace of Diamonds?

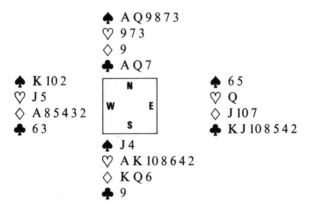

With East–West vulnerable, this was the bidding:

South	West	North	East
		1 ♠	2 ♣
2 ♡	pass	2 ♠	pass
4 ♡	pass	6 ♡	pass
pass			

The Norwegian West held the first trick with the Ace of Diamonds. Had he followed with a Club, as seems natural, it would have been impossible for South to go wrong; he would have gone up with the Ace of Clubs and eventually taken the Spade finesse. But West led another Diamond at trick 2. Trezel then played for a squeeze against East. He won the Diamond in hand, drew trumps, led a Spade to the Ace, then ran off all the trumps. Had East held both black kings, as seemed likely on the bidding, he would have been squeezed. Alas, the missing kings were divided and there was no squeeze.

At the other table the Norwegians were one down in Six Spades, as declarer lacked entries to pick up the trumps. It would have been a good hand to include in my "no swing" category, but the squeeze (or rather the lack of it!) swayed me.

The next hand is a tale of the two of Clubs, which might be entitled "Waste not, want not". The hand was played between Italy and one of the American teams in the World Olympiad of 1960. If you fancy such problems, you may like to work out at this point how the two of Clubs could be a significant card in a Spade contract.

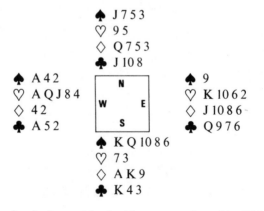

♠ J 7 5 3
♡ 9 5
◇ Q 7 5 3
♣ J 10 8

♠ A 4 2
♡ A Q J 8 4
◇ 4 2
♣ A 5 2

♠ 9
♡ K 10 6 2
◇ J 10 8 6
♣ Q 9 7 6

♠ K Q 10 8 6
♡ 7 3
◇ A K 9
♣ K 4 3

South was the dealer and both sides were vulnerable. This was the bidding when the Italians were North–South.

South	West	North	East
1 ♠	dble	2 ♠	dble
3 ♠	4 ♡	pass	pass
4 ♠	dble	pass	pass
pass			

East's double of Two Spades was "responsive", showing fair all-round values. At rubber bridge, no doubt, South would have taken his chance on beating Four Hearts, which probably goes one down as the cards lie. At duplicate small gains are more important and South was probably hoping to lose 200 or 500 in exchange for a vulnerable game.

The defence began with two rounds of Hearts, and East then switched to a trump. West won the second round of trumps and played a third round, won by dummy's Jack. Declarer now led the Jack of Clubs from the table. It is normally good technique not to cover the first honour when holding Q 9 x over J 10 x, but both defenders in fact did so, in order to impress on partner that a Club return would be safe. After the Jack of Clubs had been covered by the Queen, King and Ace, the American West returned the five of Clubs. South went up with dummy's ten and ran off the remaining trumps. This squeezed East in Clubs and Diamonds, for South's four of Clubs was a menace card against East's nine. Thus South escaped for one down.

At the other table the contract was the same and the play followed the same course up to the point at which West took the first round of Clubs with the Ace. But the Italian player led back the two of Clubs, not the five. Now East was able to defend the squeeze: he discarded all his Clubs and West's Club five took care of South's Club four.

The next hand was played by Kenneth Konstam. Konnie was no great student of technique, but when a difficult hand came along he rarely failed to play the cards in the right order:

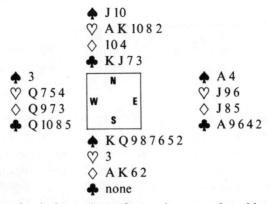

South was the dealer and North–South were vulnerable. This was the bidding:

South	West	North	East
2 ♠	pass	3 ♡	pass
3 ♠	pass	4 ♣	dble
4 ◇	pass	4 ♠	pass
6 ♠	pass	pass	pass

Had West led a Heart, a Diamond, or a Club, declarer would have made his slam with ease, but West came forth with the inspired lead of a trump. East won with the Ace and returned a trump. Now South had to find a twelfth trick. Konstam solved the problem rather neatly by leading the King of Clubs from dummy, forcing East (who had foolishly doubled Four Clubs) to cover with the Ace. Declarer ruffed and then played four more rounds of trumps.

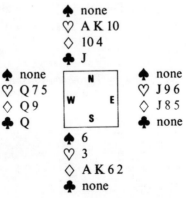

On the last Spade West discarded a Diamond and East a Heart. Then two top Diamonds squeezed West in Hearts and Clubs.

It may seem that West would have done better to have kept three Diamonds and unguarded the Hearts; but the double squeeze still works, in a different way.

I see that, a couple of years after writing up the introductory hand to this chapter, I returned to the attack on those who tried to make squeeze play sound more difficult than it really is. Often a squeeze will occur without any planning at all. Still, it helps to know what you are doing. Here is a deal which illustrates three general principles: (1) Look for a squeeze when you are in a position to win with top cards all the remaining tricks but one. (This is not an essential condition for all types of squeeze, but it tends to make the play easier.) (2) Consider whether one opponent may have to guard two suits. Aim to bring that about. (3) Failing that, look for the possibility that each opponent must guard a single suit, so that neither can control a third suit.

```
                  ♠ K Q
                  ♡ 9 7 6 3
                  ◇ K 4 2
                  ♣ 10 8 5 2
  ♠ 7 5             ┌─────────┐         ♠ 8 4
  ♡ 10 5            │    N    │         ♡ J 8 4 2
  ◇ Q 9 6        W  │    E    │         ◇ J 8 7 3
  ♣ Q J 9 7 6 3     │    S    │         ♣ A K 4
                    └─────────┘
                  ♠ A J 10 9 6 3 2
                  ♡ A K Q
                  ◇ A 10 5
                  ♣ none
```

South opens Two Clubs and North responds Two No Trumps. When North later supports Spades and indicates that he holds no ace, prospects are improved, for it becomes likely that his points are in kings and queens. South accordingly bids Seven Spades.

West's lead of the Queen of Clubs turns out badly for the defence, in a way that he cannot foresee. South ruffs, leads a Spade to the King, and ruffs another Club. Then he plays a Spade to the Queen and ruffs a third Club. By this time it is clear that the ten of Clubs is a threat against West. Three top Hearts establish that dummy's last Heart is a threat against East. Now South has the requirements for a double squeeze. He plays off all the Spade winners. At trick 10, West, playing in front of dummy, must discard a Diamond to keep his Jack of Clubs; the Club goes away from dummy and now East must also throw a Diamond, to keep his Jack of Hearts. Then South makes the last three tricks in Diamonds.

If a declarer is in Six No Trumps and has only eleven top winners, he usually has two approaches to his problem. He can give up a trick early on, to correct the timing for a possible squeeze, or he can play for a throw-in, by cashing winners first and losing a trick in the ending in the hope of a favourable return. Both ideas were tried, with mixed success, on the following hand from a multi-team event:

```
                    ♠ K Q 3
                    ♡ J 7 4
                    ◇ A J 3 2
                    ♣ 6 5 4
   ♠ 8 6             N          ♠ 10 4 2
   ♡ K 10 8 5                   ♡ 9 6 3 2
   ◇ 7 4         W      E       ◇ 10 9 8 6
   ♣ K Q J 9 2      S          ♣ 10 7
                    ♠ A J 9 7 5
                    ♡ A Q
                    ◇ K Q 5
                    ♣ A 8 3
```

South was the dealer at game-all, and at most tables the bidding went:

South	West	North	East
2 NT	pass	4 NT	pass
6 NT	pass	pass	pass

Without a Club lead there would have been time to establish the twelfth trick in Hearts, but West had a natural lead in the King of Clubs. At one table South held off and won the Club continuation. He followed with five rounds of Spades, throwing two Hearts from dummy, and then cashed four Diamond tricks. In the end position dummy held the Jack of Hearts and six of Clubs, and declarer the Ace and Queen of Hearts; West had to make a discard from K 10 of Hearts and Jack of Clubs. Naturally enough, he discarded the ten of Hearts without any outward sign of concern, and now South had to decide whether to finesse in Hearts or to play for the drop of the King. There were no real clues, but it is always more satisfactory to make a contract on a squeeze rather than on a simple finesse and declarer took the right decision.

At the other tables the South players tried the other approach. They won the opening lead and rattled off their Spade and Diamond winners. One West saved K 10 of Hearts and Queen of Clubs for his last three cards. A Club lead would have thrown him in, but instead South chose to take the Heart finesse to go one down. Another West discarded cunningly to retain King of Hearts and Q 2 of Clubs, but at this table South read the position correctly and dropped the King of Hearts. Only one West found the foolproof defence by playing his partner for the ten of Clubs. He came down to K 10 of Hearts and two of Clubs, and now, whatever declarer tried, there were only eleven tricks.

Of course, high cards can frequently be an embarrassment to a defender. This deal, from the 1972 Juan-les-Pins Bridge Festival, is a case in point and contains several other points of interest:

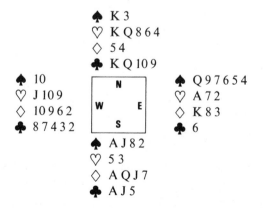

```
              ♠ K 3
              ♡ K Q 8 6 4
              ◇ 5 4
              ♣ K Q 10 9
  ♠ 10                        ♠ Q 9 7 6 5 4
  ♡ J 10 9        N           ♡ A 7 2
  ◇ 10 9 6 2    W   E         ◇ K 8 3
  ♣ 8 7 4 3 2      S          ♣ 6
              ♠ A J 8 2
              ♡ 5 3
              ◇ A Q J 7
              ♣ A J 5
```

North dealt at love-all and opened One Heart. East joined in with One Spade and there was no stopping South until Six No Trumps was reached—a distinctly optimistic contract. However, most of the high cards could be placed by East's bid, and after the lead of the ten of Spades the contract was by no means impossible. Assuming that the Diamond finesse was right, but the Ace of Hearts offside, there were eleven tricks. Declarer made his first good play when he put up the King of Spades from dummy on the first trick. The marked finesse could always be taken later, and in this way he avoided blocking the suit. At trick 2 South took a Diamond finesse and followed with a Heart to the King. East decided to hold off and declarer took a second Diamond finesse. Then he cashed the Ace of Diamonds and played off four rounds of Clubs. On the last, East found himself in trouble and was forced down to Q 9 7 of Spades and Ace of Hearts. Reading the situation exactly, South finessed the eight of Spades and got off play with a Heart to East's Ace. With only Spades left, East was forced to concede the last two tricks to South's A J of Spades.

It was an elegantly played hand but West was not pleased with his partner's defence. "Why didn't you take your Ace of Hearts when you had the chance?" he demanded aggressively. "Then you can't possibly be thrown in."

Actually, East's play was very gentlemanly—if he had won with the Ace of Hearts it would have been *West* who would have suffered the indignity of being squeezed. Suppose, after winning with the Ace, East returns a Heart. Declarer cashes all his black suit winners, taking care to end in dummy, and West is squeezed in the red suits. If, instead, East plays back a Diamond, the only difference is that South must arrange to end in hand after making his Clubs and Spades—again West is squeezed.

Bridge terminology is full of colourful expressions—South African Texas and Striped Tailed Ape spring immediately to mind—but most of them have logical explanations. For example, if a player suspects that his opponents can make a grand slam it may pay him to double the small slam that they reach *en route*. If everyone passes he makes a profit (or rather, loses less), but if the opposition redouble, the doubler beats a retreat with the speed of the striped tailed ape—reputedly a swift-moving animal.

One ending that it not so aptly named is the Suicide Squeeze.

This deal is a typical example:

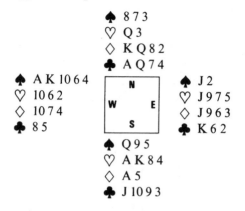

```
                        ♠ 8 7 3
                        ♡ Q 3
                        ◇ K Q 8 2
                        ♣ A Q 7 4
    ♠ A K 10 6 4          N          ♠ J 2
    ♡ 10 6 2         W         E      ♡ J 9 7 5
    ◇ 10 7 4                          ◇ J 9 6 3
    ♣ 8 5                 S           ♣ K 6 2
                        ♠ Q 9 5
                        ♡ A K 8 4
                        ◇ A 5
                        ♣ J 10 9 3
```

Suppose South deals with North–South vulnerable and opens One Heart. With no opposition bidding he reaches Three No Trumps and West leads the six of Spades to the three and Jack. As West has refrained from over-calling, South can judge that he does not have a six-card suit headed by the Ace and King, or a five-card suit together with the King of Clubs. The winning play, after taking the Queen of Spades, is to return a Spade immediately. If West does not take all his Spades, declarer has time to lose to the King of Clubs and, with the remainder of the Spades shut out, to come to at least nine tricks. If instead West cashes all his winning Spades, East is completely squeezed in three suits.

As you can see, West does not squeeze *himself* but his *partner*—hardly a suicide manœuvre. However, try the effect of changing a few low cards, thus:

```
                        ♠ 8 7 3
                        ♡ Q 3
                        ◇ K Q 8 2
                        ♣ A Q 7 4
    ♠ A K 10 6 4          N          ♠ J 2
    ♡ 10 6 5 2       W         E      ♡ J 9 7
    ◇ 10 7 4 3                        ◇ J 9 6
    ♣ none                S           ♣ K 8 6 5 2
                        ♠ Q 9 5
                        ♡ A K 8 4
                        ◇ A 5
                        ♣ J 10 9 3
```

Imagine that South is still in Three No Trumps after the same bidding. As before West leads the six of Spades and again the winning line for declarer is to take with the Queen and return the suit. This time, however, if West takes all his Spades *he* is the defender who is squeezed when declarer cashes the Ace of Clubs. Surely this is a genuine suicide squeeze?

It seems rare that you come across a hand with just one point of interest. The following deal could have been included almost anywhere in this collection of hands, for it came up in the 1973 European Championship in Ostend, it featured interesting bidding, the defenders made a fatal mistake, and a squeeze was involved in the final ending.

```
                    ♠ A 8 7 3
                    ♡ 8
                    ◇ Q J 10 8 3
                    ♣ J 10 4
  ♠ Q 10 9 6 4 2        N           ♠ none
  ♡ 7 5 3                            ♡ A Q 10 6 4
  ◇ K 9 7 6       W         E        ◇ A 5 4 2
  ♣ none               S            ♣ 8 6 3 2
                    ♠ K J 5
                    ♡ K J 9 2
                    ◇ none
                    ♣ A K Q 9 7 5
```

East dealt with East–West game and this was the bidding with Britain North–South and Poland East–West:

South	West	North	East
			pass
1 ♣	pass	1 NT	pass
2 ♣	pass	2 ♡	pass
3 ♣	pass	3 ◇	pass
3 NT	pass	4 ♣	pass
4 ◇	pass	4 ♡	pass
6 ♣	pass	pass	dble
redble	pass	pass	pass

Rose (North) and Sheehan (South) were playing Precision—which accounts for some of the bidding! Two Clubs was a form of Stayman; Two Hearts showed a Spade suit; Three Clubs and Three Diamonds were the first natural bids. Then came some cue-bids and a confident double and redouble when East decided his opponents were high enough.

I didn't know if the Poles play the Lightner slam double, but I do know that if East had announced that he was able to score an unexpected ruff against Six Clubs, even my grandmother would have led a Spade from the West seat. However, West chose to lead the five of Hearts. East took his Ace and returned a trump which South won in hand. In spite of escaping a ruff at trick 1, it looked as though South might still have to lose a Spade, but now it was East's turn to help his opponents. After declarer had ruffed a Heart in dummy he led the Queen of Diamonds and East rushed in with the Ace. After South's strong bidding it was impossible for the Ace to hold and East paid the full penalty for his thoughtless play. (Possibly he was still upset by West's failure to lead a Spade initially!) Declarer ruffed the Ace of Diamonds, ruffed the Jack of Hearts in dummy, and cashed his remaining trumps and King of Hearts. At the end West had to part with the King of Diamonds or unguard the Spades, and declarer had twelve tricks. As the contract at the other table was a pedestrian Three No Trumps, this represented a large gain for Britain who went on to win the match 12–8.

A reader once asked, "You often write about experts engineering spectacular squeezes to land slams, but how often does a squeeze occur in practice?" Well, an expert may often make a play directed towards a future squeeze, but find his play unnecessary when he discovers a friendly break or receives a helpful switch from an opponent. Often the threat of a squeeze is more significant than the squeeze itself. I am reminded of two consecutive deals from a European Championship of the 1960s where a squeeze might have featured in the play but failed to do so in the event. This was the first deal:

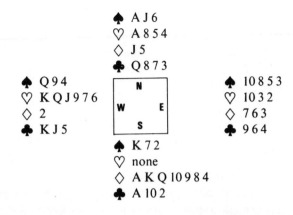

                    ♠ A J 6
                    ♡ A 8 5 4
                    ◊ J 5
                    ♣ Q 8 7 3

♠ Q 9 4   ♠ 10 8 5 3
♡ K Q J 9 7 6   N   ♡ 10 3 2
◊ 2   W   E   ◊ 7 6 3
♣ K J 5   S   ♣ 9 6 4

                    ♠ K 7 2
                    ♡ none
                    ◊ A K Q 10 9 8 4
                    ♣ A 10 2

South reached Seven Diamonds (not a good contract) after a Heart
over-call by West and the opening lead was the King of Hearts.
Declarer decided to rely on West holding the Queen of Spades
and the singleton Jack of Clubs—a line of play doomed to failure
—but to try the effect of playing West for the Queen of Spades
and K J of Clubs, surely a better chance. South ruffs the Heart in
hand, crosses to the Jack of Diamonds and ruffs a Heart. Then he
plays off five more rounds of trumps and finesses the Jack of Spades
to finish West who is in sole control of Hearts and Clubs. At the
end South holds A 10 of Clubs, North the eight of Hearts and
Queen of Clubs, and West is dead. This was the second hand:

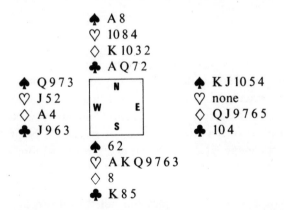

                    ♠ A 8
                    ♡ 10 8 4
                    ◊ K 10 3 2
                    ♣ A Q 7 2

♠ Q 9 7 3   ♠ K J 10 5 4
♡ J 5 2   N   ♡ none
◊ A 4   W   E   ◊ Q J 9 7 6 5
♣ J 9 6 3   S   ♣ 10 4

                    ♠ 6 2
                    ♡ A K Q 9 7 6 3
                    ◊ 8
                    ♣ K 8 5

At game-all South reached Six Hearts and West led the three of
Spades. At first sight the contract depends on finding the Clubs
3–3—it looks as though the lead has spoilt any other chances.
182

But try the effect of seven rounds of trumps; West must come down to four Clubs and the Ace of Diamonds alone, and now a Diamond lead from South establishes the twelfth trick as West has no Spades left. A good example of a squeeze without the count, you may say. Not really; we shall never know whether declarer would have found the right play, for East sacrificed in Six Spades to lose 800 points.

Having described two squeezes that never really came to pass, I was reminded of a deal from rubber bridge where declarer claimed that he had made his contract on a squeeze. South certainly made his contract but, as East stoutly maintained, with a guard in only one suit *he* wasn't squeezed. This was the hand:

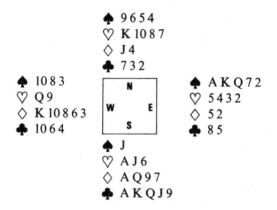

```
              ♠ 9 6 5 4
              ♡ K 10 8 7
              ◇ J 4
              ♣ 7 3 2
 ♠ 10 8 3       N        ♠ A K Q 7 2
 ♡ Q 9                   ♡ 5 4 3 2
 ◇ K 10 8 6 3  W   E     ◇ 5 2
 ♣ 10 6 4       S        ♣ 8 5
              ♠ J
              ♡ A J 6
              ◇ A Q 9 7
              ♣ A K Q J 9
```

South dealt at game-all and, playing an artificial Club system, opened One Club. North gave the negative response of One Diamond and East over-called with One Spade. Eventually South played in Five Clubs and West led the three of Spades. Declarer ruffed the second round of Spades and found the good shot of leading a low Diamond towards dummy's Jack. After some thought West went in with the King and played back a Diamond.

At the start the contract had appeared to depend on a straight guess for the Heart Queen, but now South saw other chances. It might be possible, he decided, to throw two of dummy's Hearts on winning Diamonds and so avoid a guess. With this idea in mind he drew two rounds of trumps and followed with the Ace of Diamonds to discard a Heart from dummy. However, East discarded a Spade and South was forced to change his plans. The lead sug-

gested that West had started with three Spades, so East must
have begun with a 5–4–2–2 distribution. In that case West would
be able to ruff ahead of dummy on the third round of Hearts.

Most players would have fallen back on the Heart finesse—
probably playing the defender with four Hearts for the Queen—
but South saw a better line. He trumped his good Queen of Diamonds in dummy and ruffed another Spade in hand. Then came
the last trump on which dummy threw a Heart. In order to keep
the King of Spades East had to come down to two Hearts and
now the King and Ace of Hearts were bound to drop the Queen.
South made the last trick with the Jack of Hearts.

It is true that East would have been squeezed had he held the
Queen of Hearts, but as East observed, "I never mind being
squeezed out of 5 4 3 2 in a suit!"

A number of learned articles have been written about defending
against a squeeze. Unhappily, from the average player's point of
view, much of the sound advice starts off with resounding phrases
such as "If one defender guards a two-card menace and two iso-
lated menaces, then. . . ." That usually leaves the average player
and, I regret to say, many of his peers wondering what they will
have for lunch. Nevertheless, mis-defence against squeezes can be
a costly business. Take this hand from the Ladies' European
Championship of 1965:

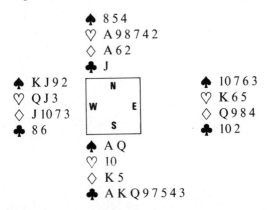

♠ 8 5 4
♡ A 9 8 7 4 2
♢ A 6 2
♣ J

♠ K J 9 2   ♠ 10 7 6 3
♡ Q J 3   ♡ K 6 5
♢ J 10 7 3   ♢ Q 9 8 4
♣ 8 6   ♣ 10 2

♠ A Q
♡ 10
♢ K 5
♣ A K Q 9 7 5 4 3

South dealt at love-all and at both tables the bidding was opened
with Two Clubs. On learning that partner held a Heart suit and

184

two Aces both declarers plunged to Seven No Trumps, arguing that the contract might well prove lay-down and at worst would depend on a finesse—good odds.

When the British ladies defended, West led a Club and after sensible discarding by East–West on the long Clubs South was forced to fall back on the losing Spade finesse to go one off. At the other table, with Rixi Markus as declarer, West chose a Diamond lead. Rixi won with dummy's Ace, cashed the Jack of Clubs and came to hand with the King of Diamonds to run the Clubs. At an early stage East parted with her Diamonds and as a result West had to let go all her Hearts in order to protect Spades and Diamonds. After the clubs came the Ace of Hearts and West had to discard from K J of Spades and Jack of Diamonds. She might have got away with it if she had dropped the Jack of Spades smoothly enough, but Rixi was alive to the situation and played the Ace of Spades to fell the now singleton King.

This one should have been easy for the defenders. All East has to do, discarding after dummy, is to retain the Hearts and Diamonds, and leave partner to look after the Spades. But it is never easy to think clearly about these things while declarer runs off an eight-card suit!

An irritating possibility when declarer is playing for a squeeze is that he may not realize that it has taken effect and still opt for a losing finesse. Sometimes correct timing can obviate the need for a guess at the end. Take this deal:

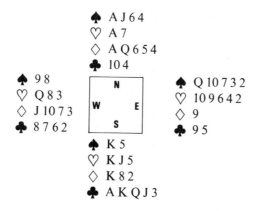

$$\spadesuit\ \text{A J 6 4}$$
$$\heartsuit\ \text{A 7}$$
$$\diamondsuit\ \text{A Q 6 5 4}$$
$$\clubsuit\ \text{10 4}$$

♠ 9 8   ♠ Q 10 7 3 2
♡ Q 8 3   ♡ 10 9 6 4 2
◇ J 10 7 3   ◇ 9
♣ 8 7 6 2   ♣ 9 5

♠ K 5
♡ K J 5
◇ K 8 2
♣ A K Q J 3

It came from a Crockfords Cup match of some years ago, where South dealt at game-all and opened Two No Trumps. After a Gerber interrogation by his partner, he ended in Seven No Trumps and West led the nine of Spades to the Jack, Queen and King.

At one table South started with five rounds of Clubs. He threw two Spades and a Diamond from dummy and West parted with a low Heart. Next came the Ace of Spades, Ace of Diamonds and King of Diamonds to reveal the bad Diamond break. Declarer cashed the Queen of Diamonds and paused to take stock. West was marked with the Jack of Diamonds; clearly East had started with five Hearts and West with three. In fact West had already been squeezed out of his Heart guard, but South did not know it; he cashed the Ace of Hearts and finessed the Jack to lose the last two tricks and 200 points.

At the other table South showed better technique. After winning with the King of Spades he tested the Diamonds immediately to learn the bad news. He cashed the third Diamond winner and followed with the Ace of Hearts, five rounds of Clubs and the Ace of Spades. At the end West was known to hold the Jack of Diamonds and East the ten of Spades, so a Heart to the King was sure to drop the Queen.

When you start to learn about squeezes, one of the first things that you are taught is that you must get the timing right. For example, suppose South plays in Six No Trumps against the lead of the King of Spades on this deal:

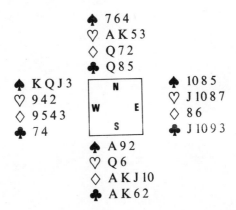

South has eleven top winners and his correct play is to hold off the opening lead. He wins the Spade continuation and cashes four rounds of Diamonds to squeeze East. But if he had won the first Spade East would have been under no pressure when the Diamonds were run off.

Straightforward enough, and the would-be squeeze expert thinks that he has finally grasped everything. But then along comes a hand like this:

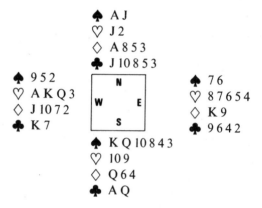

South played in Four Spades after West had doubled the opening bid of One Spade. West cashed two top Hearts and switched to a low Diamond; dummy played low. East took his King and returned a Club. Placing West with the King of Clubs (after his double), South won with the Ace and played off six rounds of trumps to squeeze West in the minor suits.

Afterwards West was suitably contrite. He suggested that if, instead of leading Hearts, he had started with a Diamond there would have been no squeeze. However, it is an odd hand. At trick 2 South wins East's Club return with the Ace, cashes the Queen of Diamonds, and again plays six rounds of trumps. At the end West has to discard from A K of Hearts, J 10 of Diamonds and King of Clubs. If he parts with a Heart, declarer can establish a trick in the suit! And any other discard gives in immediately. No fewer than two tricks are lost after the squeeze has taken effect.